MW00653953

Effective Teachers = Student Achievement

What the Research Says

James H. Stronge
College of William and Mary

EYE ON EDUCATION
6 DEPOT WAY WEST, SUITE 106
LARCHMONT, NY 10538
(914) 833–0551
(914) 833–0761 fax
www.eyeoneducation.com

Copyright © 2010 Eye On Education, Inc. All Rights Reserved.

For information about permission to reproduce selections from this book, write: Eye On Education, Permissions Dept., Suite 106, 6 Depot Way West, Larchmont, NY 10538.

Library of Congress Cataloging-in-Publication Data

Stronge, James H.

 Effective teachers = student achievement : what the research says / James H. Stronge.

  p. cm.

 ISBN 978-1-59667-154-6

 1. Effective teaching—Case studies. 2. Academic achievement—Case studies. 3. Educational innovations—Case studies. 4. School improvement programs—Case studies. I. Title.

 LB1025.3.S7886 2010

 371.102—dc22

                                                                    2010009764

10 9 8 7 6 5 4 3 2 1

The James H. Stronge Research-to-Practice Series

Evaluating What Good Teachers Do:
Eight Research-Based Standards for Assessing Teacher Excellence
James H. Stronge

Effective Teachers = Student Achievement:
What the Research Says
James H. Stronge

Student Achievement Goal Setting:
Using Data to Improve Teaching and Learning
James H. Stronge and Leslie W. Grant

The Supportive Learning Environment:
Effective Teaching Practices
Jennifer L. Hindman, James H. Stronge, and Leslie W. Grant

Planning, Instruction, and Assessment:
Effective Teaching Practices
Leslie W. Grant, Jennifer L. Hindman, and James H. Stronge

Also Available from These Authors

Handbook on Teacher Evaluation:
Assessing and Improving Performance
James H. Stronge and Pamela D. Tucker

Handbook on Educational Specialist Evaluation:
Assessing and Improving Performance
James H. Stronge and Pamela D. Tucker

Handbook on Teacher Portfolios for Evaluation
and Professional Development
Pamela Tucker, James Stronge, and Christopher Gareis

Other Great Titles from Eye On Education

Leading School Change: 9 Strategies to Bring *Everybody* On Board
Todd Whitaker

Classroom Walkthroughs to Improve Teaching and Learning
Donald S. Kachur, Judith A. Stout, and Claudia L. Edwards

Help Teachers Engage Students: Action Tools for Administrators
Annette Brinkman, Gary Forlini, and Ellen Williams

About the Author

James H. Stronge is the Heritage Professor in the Educational Policy, Planning, and Leadership Area at the College of William and Mary, Williamsburg, Virginia. His research interests include policy and practice related to teacher quality, and teacher and administrator evaluation. His work on teacher quality focuses on how to identify effective teachers and how to enhance teacher effectiveness. Dr. Stronge has presented his research at state, national, and international conferences, such as those conducted by the American Educational Research Association, American Association of School Administrators, Asia-Pacific Conference on Gifted, Association for Supervision and Curriculum Development, European Council of International Schools, National Evaluation Institute, and University Council for Educational Administration. Additionally, he has worked extensively with local school districts and other educational organizations on issues related to teacher effectiveness, teacher selection, and teacher and administrator evaluation.

Stronge has authored, coauthored, or edited twenty-two books and more than one hundred articles, chapters, and technical reports. Selected books have been translated and published in Arabic, Mandarin, Italian, Korean, Portuguese, and Vietnamese. Some of his recent books include:

- *Student Achievement Goal Setting: Using Data to Improve Teaching and Learning* (Eye On Education, 2009)

- *Qualities of Effective Principals* (Association for Supervision and Curriculum Development, 2008)

- *Qualities of Effective Teaching*, 2nd ed. (Association for Supervision and Curriculum Development, 2007)

- *The Teacher Quality Index: A Protocol for Teacher Selection* (Association for Supervision and Curriculum Development, 2006)

- *Teacher Pay and Teacher Quality: Attracting, Developing, and Retaining the Best Teachers* (Corwin Press, 2006)

- *Linking Teacher Evaluation and Student Achievement* (Association for Supervision and Curriculum Development, 2005)

- *Evaluating Teaching*, 2nd ed. (Corwin Press, 2005)

Dr. Stronge has been a teacher, counselor, and district-level administrator. His doctorate is in educational administration and planning from the University of Alabama. He may be contacted at: The College of William and Mary, School of Education, PO Box 8795, Williamsburg, VA 23187-8795; 757-221-2339; or http://wmpeople.wm.edu/jhstro.

Acknowledgements

I would like to express my gratitude to a number of individuals who offered value insight into the creation and development of *Effective Teachers = Student Achievement*. First, Dr. Leslie Grant and Dr. Patricia Popp, both from the College of William and Mary, and Dr. Catherine Little, University of Connecticut (Storrs), helped form and refine the ideas in the book through our collaboration on a variety of research and writing projects. As we have continued to collaborate on research endeavors related to teacher effectiveness, Leslie, Pat, and Catherine have proven to be inspirational and innovative partners in our efforts to expand our understanding of what makes good teachers good. In fact, each in her own right is a highly capable and respected teacher of teachers.

Next, I would like to thank another colleague from the College of William and Mary, Dr. Thomas Ward. Tom and I have partnered on a number of funded projects in which we focused on the impact of teachers on student achievement and what effective teachers do. Tom's expertise as a research methodologist and statistician has been invaluable, particularly in the application of hierarchical linear modeling and other regression models in our analyses of teacher effects on student achievement.

Dr. Marco Muñoz, Evaluation Specialist for Jefferson County Public Schools, Kentucky, on various occasions provided his expertise in reviewing and editing various journal articles related to teacher effectiveness and value-added analysis. Once again, Marco generously provided a careful review and offered his insights for improvement of this manuscript. The book is significantly strengthened because of his most helpful contributions.

Finally, I wish to express my gratitude to Xianxuan Xu. Xian currently is a Ph.D. candidate in the College of William and Mary's Educational Policy, Planning, and Leadership Program and my graduate assistant. She contributed to *Effective Teachers = Student Achievement* in substantial measure through her help with the background review of the extant value-added research, her drafting of the annotations included in Part II, and her coauthoring of Chapter 4. Xian is an extraordinarily talented young educator who promises to make significant contributions to our understanding of teaching and teacher quality during her career, particularly in terms of international comparative analyses focusing on teachers in the United States and China. She aspires to return to her native China as a university professor following the completion of her doctoral work, and I am convinced that the university that selects her will be fortunate, indeed.

To everyone who contributed, I wish to express my admiration for your dedicated work as educators and my appreciation for helping make this book a reality. Ultimately, I wish to acknowledge, you, the readers of previous works that I have written, including such books as *Qualities of Effective Teachers*. Thank you for having the confidence to embrace another of my writing projects.

Contents

Introduction

Too many times we have seen purported educational innovations foisted on our teachers and students and then, just as rapidly as the "innovations" appeared, they disappeared. These reforms didn't last because they didn't work. No evidence, no support.

Ultimately, the value and validity of claims that teachers matter most rest on the evidence that supports the claims. Do teachers make a difference in children's lives? If so, how much and how important are those differences? Is the impact of an effective—or ineffective—teacher durable? Can reform succeed without, first, addressing teacher quality? These are the teacher effectiveness issues that *Teacher Effectiveness = Student Achievement: What the Research Says* seeks to illuminate.

Conceptual Framework for the Book

In *Teacher Effectiveness = Student Achievement: What the Research Says* I provide in terms as clear and compelling as I can that teachers do, indeed, matter most when it comes to school improvement and student learning. The premise of the book is that among myriad factors within our schools, there is no more powerful influence on student success than the teacher.

In an effort to elucidate this simple truth, the book is organized around a series of interlocking questions related to the connection between teacher effectiveness and student achievement. The following graphic offers a conceptual framework for *Effective Teachers = Student Achievement*:

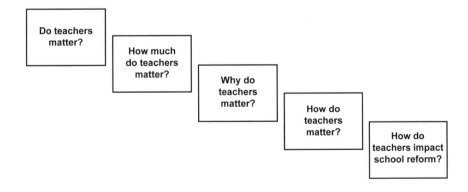

What is intended by this step-wise progress of questions is that, from beginning to end, teachers play a dynamic and central role in school reform and student achievement.

Research Basis for the Book

How Do We Know the Impact of Teachers on Student Achievement?

The primary basis for exploring issues of teacher effectiveness in *Effective Teachers = Student Achievement* is the value-added teacher assessment research that has emerged in the past decade or two. Value-added studies can be undertaken with various statistical methods, for example, hierarchical linear modeling (HLM) or the mixed model method pioneered by William Sanders in the Tennessee Value-Added Assessment System. Regardless of the statistical approach used, what is essential is that the influence of the teacher be teased out and separated from other influences on student performance. For example, in HLM analyses a host of predictor variables can be controlled for, such as prior student achievement, reading ability, days absent, free and reduced lunch. In Sander's mixed model Tennessee Value-Added Assessment System, the student's prior achievement is the only control variable because Sander's purports that the student's prior performance absorbs most of the other influences on performance. Again, what is essential is that the teacher's influence be separated from other influences on student achievement if we are to understand and measure the teacher's impact:

Value-added is often confused with simple growth because the words themselves make it is easy to think about this growth as the "value" that is "added" over the last year. But the statistical method known as "value-added assessment," as developed for the state of Tennessee by William Sanders when he was a professor of statistics at the state university, is a way of isolating the impact of instruction on student learning. Its great advantage is its ability to separate the annual academic growth of students into two parts: that that can be attributed to the student and that which can be attributed to the classroom, school, or district (Hershberg, 2005, p. 280).

How Do We Know What Teachers Do Impacts Student Achievement?

Even if we are able to discern the impact of teachers on student learning, it isn't enough. If this is all we can know, it's like giving me a report card and telling me I'm good, bad, or indifferent. Although it may be helpful to categorize me as effective or ineffective, that fact alone won't make be a better teacher. Rather, I need to know what good teachers do and then how to get better. Consequently, there must be a second stage to value-added research. Once we analyze the effectiveness of a teacher, we must be able to go inside the classroom and discover what the most effectively teachers do that is different from their not-so-effective colleagues.

Another way to think about this second stage of value-added research and teacher effectiveness is that we need to understand *what* the effective teacher does, not just *what is the effect* of the teacher. And what we really are interested in is stepping inside the black box of the mysterious classroom and demystifying the power and practices of effective teachers. This is precisely what is included in *Effective Teachers = Student Achievement*, particularly in Chapter 4 in which the guiding question is: What do effective teachers do?

To the Reader

I trust that readers of *Effective Teachers = Student Achievement* will find the research synthesis presented in its pages a compelling story. My intent is to illuminate as brightly as possible why the quality of our teachers is so extraordinarily important to the lives of students—not just now, but for their future well-being, as well. We've always known, at least intuitively, that teachers matter inordinately to students' lives. Now we know empirically.

Part I

Effective Teachers = Student Achievement

1

Do Teachers Matter? The Impact of Teachers on Student Achievement

...[T]eacher quality matters—and...it matters a great deal. If we are committed to this premise, then we must be committed to populating our schools with the highest quality teachers possible.

— Stronge, Gareis, & Little (2006, p. 2)

Do teachers matter? Absolutely—and a great deal. In fact, among the factors within our control as educators, teachers offer the greatest opportunity for improving the quality of life of our students. As noted in *How the World's Best-Performing School Systems Come Out on Top*, an international study comparing data from the Organization for Economic Co-operation and Development's (OECD) Programme for International Student Assessment (PISA), "The quality of an education system cannot exceed the quality of its teachers" (Barber & Mourshed, 2007, p. iii).

If we want to improve the quality of our schools and positively affect the lives of our students, we must change the quality of our teaching. This is our best hope to systematically and dramatically improve education. Although we can reform the curriculum, ultimately, it is teachers who implement it; although we can provide professional development on new instructional strategies, ultimately, it is teachers who deploy them; although we can focus on data analysis of student performance, ultimately, it is teachers who produce the results we are analyzing.

The focus of *Effective Teachers = Student Achievement* is just that: Teachers do matter extraordinarily in terms of both school improvement and student success. In addressing the overarching question of whether teachers matter in this opening chapter, I focus on three concomitant questions:

- ♦ What is the evidence that teachers matter to student achievement?

- ♦ Where do student achievement differences occur—at the school or teacher level?

- ♦ What are the possibilities and pitfalls of estimating teacher effects on student achievement?

What Is the Evidence that Teachers Matter to Student Achievement?

Consider the following findings:

- ♦ Teacher effectiveness is the dominant factor influencing student academic growth (Sanders & Rivers, 1996; Wright, Horn, & Sanders, 1997).

- ♦ A post hoc analysis of achievement test gains indicated that the gains made by students taught by exemplary teachers outpaced expected levels of growth (Allington & Johnston, 2000).

- ♦ Value-added estimates of teacher quality are not correlated to student initial test scores. This means an effective teacher performs well among both low- and high-ability students, whereas an ineffective teacher is ineffective with both types of students (Aaronson, Barrow, & Sander, 2007).

These sobering findings are derived from assessments of the teacher's measurable impact on student achievement using value-added methodologies. Over the past several years, numerous researchers have explored the "value-added effects" of a particular school or teacher through the use of sophisticated statistical models involving longitudinal data on student achievement. These value-added methods have the advantage of removing the effects of factors not under the control of the school, such as prior student achievement and socioeconomic status, and thereby providing more accurate estimates of school or teacher effectiveness. This statistical modeling approach has taken a number of forms and each generated differential statistical power of teacher effects (Palardy & Rumberger, 2008; Rowan, Correnti, & Miller, 2002). However, the bottom-line findings of all these value-added studies are that teachers matter and teacher quality is the most significant schooling factor impacting student learning. This impact is not just of statistical significance; more importantly, it is of practical significance.

Statistical Significance Versus Practical Significance

In educational research, statistical significance is used to determine if certain observed differences exist beyond a chance occurrence. However, statistical significance does not determine the magnitude of the differences or the likelihood of obtaining similar results in the future. On the other hand, practical significance refers to the fact that the research findings can be viewed as information of value to teachers, school administrators, policy makers, and others who are involved in day-to-day educational practice (Gall, 2001). Practical significance indicates that results are of a magnitude that would make a real-world difference.

William Sanders pioneered a widely used statistical approach, initially referred to as the Tennessee Value-Added Assessment System (TVAAS), for determining the effectiveness of school systems, schools, and teachers based on student academic growth over time. An integral part of TVAAS is a massive, longitudinally merged database linking student outcomes to the schools and systems in which they are enrolled, and to the teachers to whom they are assigned, as the students transition from grade to grade. Research conducted using data from the TVAAS database has shown that ethnicity, socioeconomic level, class size, and classroom heterogeneity are poor predictors of student academic growth. Rather, based on these studies, the effectiveness of the teacher is the major determinant of student academic progress (Wright, Horn, & Sanders, 1997).

The available evidence suggests that the main driver of the variation in student learning at school is the quality of the teachers.... Studies that take into account all of the available evidence of teacher effectiveness suggest that students placed with high-performing teachers will progress three times as fast as those placed with low-performing teachers. (Barber & Mourshed, 2007, p. 12)

After controlling for prior student achievement, the TVAAS studies found the impact of teachers on student achievement to be directly related to the effectiveness of the teachers, themselves.

Regardless of initial achievement level, teachers in the top quintile facilitated desirable academic progress for *all* students. However, regardless of their entering achievement levels, students under the tutelage of teachers in the bottom quintile made unsatisfactory gains. As the teacher effectiveness quintile increased, lower-achieving students were first to benefit, followed by average students and, lastly, by students considerably above average (Sanders & Rivers, 1996, p. 7).

Moreover,

- ineffective teachers were found to be ineffective with all students, regardless of their prior achievement level.

- the average teachers facilitated achievement gains with lower achieving students, but not higher student achievers.

- highly effective teachers were generally effective with all student achievement levels. (Sanders & Rivers, 1996)

Evidence of Teacher Impact on Student Learning

As demonstrated in the TVAAS studies, teacher effectiveness can be captured by measured student achievement gains. In fact, numerous studies have found similar effects on student learning for effective versus ineffective teachers. Consider the outcomes of teacher effectiveness on student achievement drawn from a sampling of studies presented in Figure 1.1 below.

Figure 1.1. Summary Findings of Teacher Effects on Student Achievement from Selected Studies

Study	Key Findings
Emmer & Evertson (1979)	◆ Study results indicated strong teacher effects on pupil attitudes in both mathematics and English.
	◆ Teacher effects on pupil achievement varied depending upon subject matter and class means for initial achievement level.
Sanders & Rivers, (1996); Wright, Horn, & Sanders, (1997)	◆ Students of different ethnic groups respond equivalently within the same level of teacher effectiveness.
	◆ Classroom context variables of heterogeneity among students have relatively little influence on academic gain.

Study	Key Findings
Hanushek, Kain, & Rivkin (1998)	♦ Lower-bound estimates suggest that variations in teacher quality account for at least 7.5 percent of the total variation in measured achievement gains, and there are reasons to believe that the true percentage is considerably larger.
Mendro, Jordan, Gomez, Anderson, & Bembry (1998a, 1998b)	♦ The research findings in these studies on teacher effectiveness found not only that teachers have large effects on student achievement, but also that the measures of effectiveness are stable over time.
Allington & Johnston (2000)	♦ The exemplary teachers produced the kinds of student literacy achievement that is beyond even the most sophisticated standardized tests. This means the student achievement growth (either intellectual development or social development) and the conception of exemplary teaching cannot be fully captured by standardized test scores.
Nye, Konstantopoulos, & Hedges (2004)	♦ The variance of teacher effects in mathematics is much larger than that in reading. This finding may be because math is mostly learned in school and, therefore, may be more directly influenced by teachers. Also, this finding might be a result of greater variation in how well teachers teach mathematics.
Rockoff (2004)	♦ Drawing from a data set of approximately 10,000 students, Rockoff found that a one-standard-deviation increase in teacher quality raises student test scores by approximately 0.1 standard deviation in reading and math on nationally standardized distributions of achievement.
Rivkin, Hanushek, & Kain (2005)	♦ A one-standard-deviation increase in average teacher quality for a grade raises average student achievement in the grade by at least 0.11 standard deviation of the total test score distribution in math and 0.09 standard deviation in reading.

Study	Key Findings
Aaronson, Barrow, & Sander (2007)	♦ Estimates of teacher effects are relatively stable over time, reasonably impervious to a variety of conditioning variables, and do not appear to be driven by classroom sorting (i.e., student/teacher assignment) or selective use of test scores.
Stronge, Ward, Tucker, & Hindman (2008)	♦ Based on prediction models developed through the use of regression analyses with third-grade teachers, most students' actual achievement scores were within a close range of their predicted scores. However, teacher effectiveness scores ranged from more than a standard deviation above predicted performance to more than a standard deviation below, indicating a wide dispersion of teacher effectiveness.
	♦ Teachers who were highly effective in producing higher-than-expected student achievement gains (top quartile) in one end-of-course content test (reading, math, science, social studies) tended to produce top quartile residual gain scores in all four content areas. Teachers who were ineffective (bottom quartile) in one content area tended to be ineffective in all four content areas.

A Case Study of Teacher Impact on Student Achievement

In a study of three school districts from a state in the southeastern United States, a group of colleagues and I assessed teacher effectiveness in terms of student learning gains (Stronge, Ward, Tucker, & Grant, In review). We defined effective teachers as those teachers whose students made gains in the top quartile on reading and mathematics standardized achievement tests; less-effective teachers were defined as those teachers whose students made gains in the bottom quartile. The measures of student achievement were the math and reading scores from the selected state's end-of-grade tests.

A regression-based methodology, hierarchical linear model (HLM), was used to estimate the growth for all students included in the sample in order to predict the expected achievement level for each individual child. Figures 1.2 and 1.3 (page 10) provide a graphical representation of the predicated and actual achievement scores of the 4,600 fifth-grade students.

Hierarchical Linear Modeling

Hierarchical linear model (HLM) is a sophisticated form of regression analysis that can account for the influence of individual, class-level, school-level, and other variables on an outcome such as student achievement. HLM allows examination of association among multilevel, nested data—for instance, students nested within classrooms nested within schools. With longitudinal (e.g., three-year) data, HLM can be helpful in predicting student achievement within schools and classrooms. Additionally, HLM can statistically block the impact exerted by non–school/teacher-level factors and, thus, enable an exhaustive examination on the effect of schools and teachers on student academic performance.

Figure 1.2. Scatterplot for Fifth-Grade Student Predicted Versus Actual Reading Achievement Indices

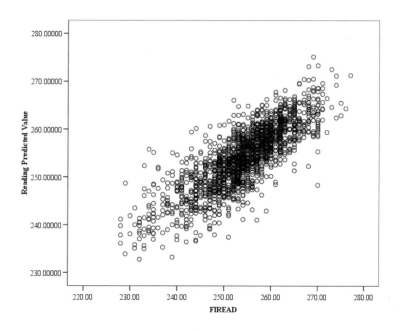

Figure 1.3. Scatterplot for Fifth-Grade Student Predicted Versus Actual Mathematics Achievement Indices

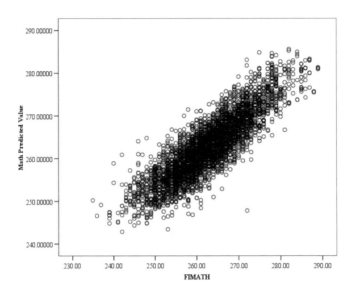

Following the HLM analysis of the approximately 4,600 students' predicted and actual test scores on reading and math, estimates of teacher impact on achievement (referred to as Teacher Achievement Indices [TAI]) were calculated by averaging all student residual gain scores for the 307 teachers included in the study. After controlling for variables such as class size, prior student achievement, and a host of individual student variables (e.g., gender, ethnicity, socioeconomic level, English as a Second Language learners), the students residual gain scores (difference between predicted and actual achievement levels) were calculated. The students were then traced back to the teachers responsible for teaching them reading and math, respectively, and gain scores were aggregated at the teacher level, producing a TAI. Finally, the TAI values were standardized on a T-scale (mean = 50, SD = 10) for ease of interpretation. As indicated in Figures 1.4 (Reading) and 1.5 (Mathematics), the Teacher Effectiveness Indices scores (mean residual gains for students assigned to given teachers) ranged from approximately two standard deviations below expectations to two standard deviations above expectations.

Figure 1.4. Teacher Effectiveness Indices (TAI) Distribution for Reading

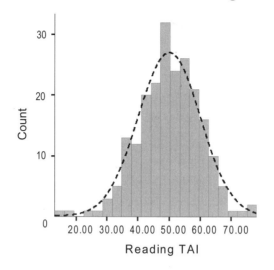

Figure 1.5. Teacher Effectiveness Indices (TAI) Distribution for Mathematics

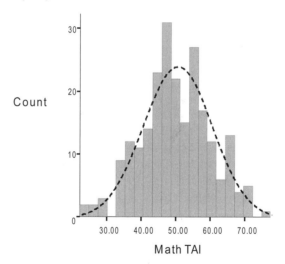

This amount of variability in teacher effectiveness means that the quality of the teacher that a student happens to be assigned to will play an extraordinary role in the student's academic success, at least during the time the student is under the teacher's tutelage, and perhaps even beyond. (This latter idea of impact of beyond the time spent with a teacher—residual effect—is explored in Chapter 2.)

Where Do Student Achievement Differences Occur: At the School or Teacher Level?

There are large differences among schools in their impact on student achievement. "School quality is an important determinant of academic performance and an important tool for raising the achievement of low income students" (Hanushek, Kain, & Rivkin, 1998, p. 31). In fact, the between school variance accounts for 3.3 percent and 5.5 percent of the variance in reading and math achievement, respectively. However, the within-school-between-grade variance accounts for 8.9 percent and 15.3 percent of variance in reading and math achievement—approximately three times as great as the differences noted between schools. In practical terms, this means there is more variability in teacher quality within classrooms than across schools. It also suggests that "while schools have powerful effects on student achievement differences, these effects appear to derive most importantly from variations in teacher quality" (Hanushek, Kain, & Rivkin, 1998, p. 1). In other words, heterogeneity in teacher effectiveness dominates school quality differences and is a significant source of student achievement variations.

Interestingly, "resource differences explain at most a small part of the difference in school quality, raising serious doubts that additional expenditures would substantially raise achievement under the current institutional structure" (Hanushek, Kain, & Rivkin, 1998, p. 31). Rather than the overall school organization, leadership, or even financial conditions, heterogeneity among teachers is the most significant source of achievement variations. Thus, there is a much greater opportunity to improve student performance by focusing on teacher quality and teacher performance than by focusing on any other school-related means.

Factors Influencing Student Achievement

After conducting an extensive review of the extant literature on teacher effects on student achievement, an Australian researcher, John Hattie, in *Teachers Make a Difference: What Is the Research Evidence?* (2003) proposed six major sources that can account for the variance in students' academic achievement (Figure 1.6):

- ◆ *Student* (i.e., prior student achievement, aptitude, motivation, effort), which may account for approximately 50 percent of the variance of achievement;

- ◆ *Home* (i.e., family support and encouragement for learning, economic advantages or disadvantages, involvement with school), which may account for approximately 5 to 10 percent of the variance;

- *Schools* (i.e., resources, quality of facilities, academic focus, learning culture), which may account for approximately 5 to 10 percent of the variance;

- *Principals,* whose influence is already accounted for under the "Schools" category;

- *Peer effects,* which may account for approximately 5 to 10 percent of the variance;

- *Teachers,* which may account for approximately 30 percent of the variance.

Variance

Variance is a commonly used measure of variability (which is also known as individual differences). For instance, in educational research, variance can be used to measure the amount of difference in students' achievement scores around the mean score. The desire to understand what factors account for the variability in student academic performance plays a central role in educational research design (Gall, Gall, & Borg, 2007).

Figure 1.6. Estimated Influence of Factors Accounting for Variations in Student Achievement

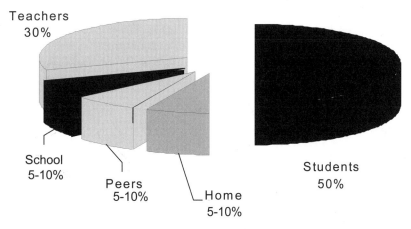

Teachers
30%

School
5-10%

Peers
5-10%

Home
5-10%

Students
50%

Taken from Hattie, 2003.

Given other studies reporting on factors affecting the variability of student achievement,[1] Hattie may have overstated the direct influence of teachers on student learning. Nonetheless, his point is quite clear: When it comes to improving student achievement, placing the spotlight on teachers and their *direct* (i.e., proximal factors) work with students yields far greater benefits than putting the resources into *indirect* (i.e., distal factors) school-level reforms.

School Versus Home Influences on Student Achievement

The reality is that various factors affecting student success—the student, home, school, teacher, other influences—are overlapping and interactive. Student achievement is not just subject to teacher effects alone; they also are impacted by family background and many other factors (Leigh, n.d.). Thus, it is virtually impossible to parse out the precise impact of any given factor on the subtle and substantial complexities of student learning. However, we certainly can attempt to approximate these influences.

In estimating the influence of home versus school, Dan Goldhaber (2002) "found that the vast majority (about 60 percent) of the differences in student test scores are explained by individual and family background characteristics" (p. 2). His colleagues and he also noted that the total set of influences of a school, including school, teacher, and class-level variables accounted for approximately 21 percent of the variation in student achievement (a smaller percentage than that estimated by Hattie in Figure 1.6, page 13). He also noted that:

> This 21 percent is composed mainly of characteristics that were not directly quantified in the analyses. Since we used statistical models that included many observable school-, teacher-, and class-level variables—such as school and class size, teachers' levels of education and experience, and schools' demographic makeup—it is clear that the things that make schools and teachers effective defy easy measurement. (Goldhaber, n.d., p. 2)

School Versus Teacher Influences on Student Achievement

Variance because of differences among teachers is substantial in comparison to the variance between schools. Much of the teacher quality variation exists *within* rather than *between* schools (Nye, Konstantopoulos, & Hedges, 2004; Rivkin, Hanushek, & Kain, 2005).

In a study where students and teachers were randomly assigned to classrooms, the portion of variance in student achievement in grade 2 reading that can be attributed to differences in teacher effectiveness is more than twice as

1 Studies that estimate the amount of variability in student achievement accounted for by teacher effects are reported on in Chapter 2.

large as the portion that can be attributed to variations in overall school effectiveness. The contrast is even sharper for reading in grade 3, with the individual teacher effectiveness variable three times as large as the overall school effectiveness variable. This suggests that naturally occurring teacher effects are typically larger than naturally occurring school effects (Nye, Konstantopoulos, & Hedges, 2004). Which teacher a student happens to get within a school matters more than which school the student happens to attend (Nye, Konstantopoulos, & Hedges, 2004).

Palardy and Rumberger (2008) further note that when we separate teacher effects from school effects, the effect size estimates for the teacher are substantial. The reason is that between-school variance can be attributed to the heterogeneity of teacher effectiveness across schools. The research usually assumes that the source of between-school effects on student achievement to be principal leadership, school climate, and other nonteacher factors. But the reality is that teachers are not randomly assigned to schools. The cream of the teacher population is usually attracted to schools with higher pay and better working conditions.[2] Thus, the difference in the mean effectiveness of teachers across schools also contributes to the between-school variance.

Another interesting finding is that the variation in student socioeconomic status cannot explain the variance of teacher effectiveness within schools (Nye, Konstantopoulos, & Hedges, 2004). This means an effective teacher is effective with all students, regardless of their socioeconomic background, whereas an ineffective teacher is ineffective with all students. Given these findings regarding the powerful impact of teacher effectiveness, and because teacher effects are found to be larger than school effects, educational policies focusing on teacher effects on student achievement will be more promising than policies focusing on school effects (Nye et al., 2004).

What Are the Possibilities and Pitfalls of Estimating Teacher Effects on Student Achievement?

For the last decade or more, research on Value-Added Methods (VAMs) of teacher effectiveness has received increasing attention and support in the broader educational community. VAMs typically employed various regression analyses, such as HLM, on longitudinal student achievement data to determine the magnitude of influences exerted by schools, teachers, the student background characteristics, and other related factors.

VAMs are perceived by some researchers to be an unbiased and reliable approach for estimating the effectiveness of individual teachers based on their students' achievement gains (Wright, Horn, & Sanders, 1997). These

---

2 The issue of teacher effectiveness and teacher pay is addressed in more detail in Chapter 5.

methods have the advantage of removing the influences of factors not under the control of the school/teacher, such as prior student achievement and socioeconomic status, thereby providing more accurate estimates of school or teacher effectiveness.

Although the emerging use of value-added models in the field of education is yielding interesting and valuable finding for us to consider, the methods are not without flaws. "Value-added models are providing us with new information about teachers, information that we've never had before… but the information we get from value-added modeling is not perfect information" (Hannaway, cited in Viadero, 2008a, p. 13). Measuring educational variables such as teacher effects on student achievement is complex work, and we simply don't have the precision we need—with value-added or any other means, for that matter. Because value-added methodology is central to the book, a fuller discussion of the possibilities and pitfalls of VAM is provided in Part II.

Conclusion

So, do teachers matter? In terms of impact on students as well as impact on school improvement, yes, teachers matter. In fact, if we attempt to reform education without focusing on the classroom, the effort likely will be superfluous at best. As Hattie (2003) noted:

> Interventions at the structural, home, policy, or school level is like searching for your wallet which you lost in the bushes, under the lamppost because that is where there is light. The answer lies elsewhere—it lies in the person who gently closes the classroom door and performs the teaching act— the person who puts into place the end effects of so many policies, who interprets these policies, and who is alone with students during their 15,000 hours of schooling. (pp. 2–3)

Reform occurs one classroom at a time. When teachers get better, schools get better. Indeed, there is no other formula for school improvement. Why? Because teachers matter most.

2

How Much Do Teachers Matter?

Teachers have large effects on student achievement…and the effects teachers have are on an order of magnitude which dwarfs the effects associated with curriculum, staff development, restructuring, and other types of educational interventions.

— Mendro, Jordan, Gomez, Anderson, & Bembry (1998a, p. 1)

If we accept the premise that teachers matter significantly to student learning and school improvement, the question remains: *How much do they matter?* Is the difference between effective and ineffective teachers enough to be of practical concern and redirect public policy? Does the difference in teacher quality justify investing our scarce resources in finding and keeping the best teachers? This chapter discusses the overarching issue of how much teachers matter to student achievement. The following guiding questions are addressed:

◆ How influential is teacher effectiveness on student achievement?

◆ How much of the variability in student achievement can be explained by teacher effectiveness?

◆ What are practical implications of teacher effects on student achievement?

♦ How can teacher effects help with equity for all students?

How Influential Is Teacher Effectiveness on Student Achievement?

How does the impact of effective teachers compare to that of ineffective teachers? In a value-added impact study of teachers in the Dallas, Texas, Public Schools, the research team found that teacher effectiveness is strongly related to student outcomes (Jordan, Mendro, & Weerasinghe, 1997). More precisely, the differential impact of effective versus ineffective teachers on student success was striking:

♦ Students with no Quintile 1 (bottom 20 percentile teachers, i.e., least effective) teacher would have a 7 in 10 chance of being in the top half of effect size distribution.

♦ Students with no Quintile 5 (top 20 percentile teachers, i.e., most effective) teacher would have a 2 in 3 chance of being in the bottom half of effect size distribution.

♦ With no Quintile 1 (least effective) teacher, students would have less than a 1 in 10 chance of being in the bottom 20 percent of effect size distribution.

♦ With no Quintile 5 (most effective) teacher, students would have less than a 1 in 6 chance of being in the top 20 percent of effect size distribution.

Effect Size

Effect size is a measure of the magnitude of a treatment effect. Effect size helps us determine if the treatment effect is practically significant. The effect size can be interpreted as the average percentile standing of the students who received treatment relative to the average untreated students. For instance, in a study by Nye, Konstantopoulos, and Hedges (2004), having a teacher from the top quadrant (75th percentile) was found to have an effect size of 0.48 on student achievement in mathematics. Using a z score to translate an effect size of 0.48 would result in the mean achievement of students taught by top quartile teachers being at the 68th percentile as compared with the 50th percentile for students taught by average effectiveness teachers.

Effective Versus Ineffective Teachers: Studies Involving Primary Level Students

Using data from the Tennessee Value-Added System, the research team of Nye, Konstantopoulos, and Hedges (2004) found there are substantial differences among teachers in their ability to produce achievement gains in their students. If primary grade teacher effects are normally distributed, these findings would suggest that the difference in achievement gains between having a 25th percentile teacher (a not so effective teacher) and a 75th percentile teacher (an effective teacher) is more than one-third of a standard deviation in reading and almost half a standard deviation in mathematics. Similarly, the difference in achievement gains between having a 50th percentile teacher (an average teacher) and a 90th percentile teacher (a very effective teacher) is approximately one-third of a standard deviation in reading and somewhat smaller than half a standard deviation in mathematics (Figure 2.1).

Figure 2.1. Comparative Impact of Effective Versus Ineffective Primary Grade Teachers

Teacher Effectiveness Level	Comparative Impact on Student Achievement
◆ Reading: 25th vs. 75th percentile teacher	+0.35 Standard Deviation
◆ Math: 25th vs. 75th percentile teacher	+0.48 Standard Deviation
◆ Reading: 50th vs. 90th percentile teacher	+0.33 Standard Deviation
◆ Reading: 50th vs. 90th percentile teacher	+0.46 Standard Deviation

In an Australian value-added study, the researcher analyzed data that covered more than 10,000 Australian primary school teachers and more than 90,000 pupils to estimate teacher effectiveness. Teacher output/teacher effectiveness was measured by the score gains made by the students they taught in a second standardized test, as compared to the first test that had taken place two years earlier. Based on the findings, teachers had a significant impact on student achievement gains. After adjusting for measurement error, the resulting teacher fixed effects were widely dispersed across teachers (Leigh, n.d.):

♦ Moving from a teacher at the 25th percentile to a teacher at the 75th percentile would raise test scores by one-seventh of a standard deviation. A 0.5 standard deviation increase in student test scores is equivalent to a full year's learning. This implies that a 75th percentile teacher can achieve in three-quarters of a year what a 25th percentile teacher can achieve in a full year (p. 11) (Figure 2.2).

Figure 2.2. Time Needed to Achieve the Same Amount of Student Learning with 75th Percentile Versus 25th Percentile Effectiveness Teachers

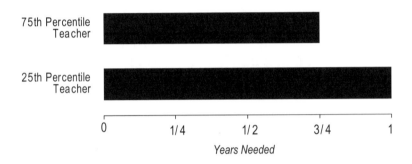

Time in School Year Needed to Achieve the Same Amount of Learning

♦ Moving from a teacher at the 10th percentile to a teacher at the 90th percentile would raise test scores by one-quarter of a standard deviation. This implies that a teacher at the 90th percentile can achieve in half a year what a teacher at the 10th percentile can achieve in a full year (p. 11) (Figure 2.3).

Figure 2.3. Time Needed to Achieve the Same Amount of Student Learning with 90th Percentile Versus 10th Percentile Effectiveness Teachers

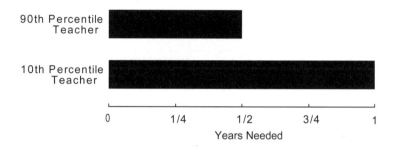

Time in School Year Needed to Achieve the Same Amount of Learning

Effective Versus Ineffective Teachers: Studies Involving Upper Elementary/Middle Level Students

In a study of teacher effectiveness involving fifth-grade teachers, the research team considered the implications of having a top- versus bottom-quartile (75th percentile versus 25th percentile in effectiveness as measured by ability to raise student achievement scores) teacher in terms of student gains. When end-of-course fifth-grade scores were considered and gain scores calculated, the differences were substantial. For reading, students taught by bottom-quartile teachers could expect to score, on average, at the 21st percentile on the state's reading assessment, whereas students taught by the top-quartile teachers could expect to score at approximately the 54th percentile (Figure 2.4, page 22). We found similar results for mathematics, with the students in the bottom-quartile teachers' classrooms scoring, on average, at the 38th percentile; students in the top-quartile teachers' classrooms scored at the 70th percentile (Figure 2.5, page 22). In both reading and math, there were no statistically significant differences in student achievement levels at the beginning of the school year between the top- and bottom-quartile teachers' classes. Thus, this 30-plus percentile point difference was attributed to the quality of teaching occurring in the classrooms during one academic year (Stronge, Ward, Tucker, & Grant, In review).

Figure 2.4. Percentile Differences in Student Reading Achievement following 1 Year of Instruction in Top- Versus Bottom-Quartile Teachers' Classes

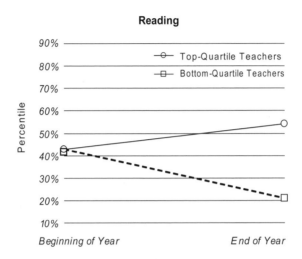

Figure 2.5. Percentile Differences in Student Mathematics Achievement following 1 Year of Instruction in Top- Versus Bottom-Quartile Teachers' Classes

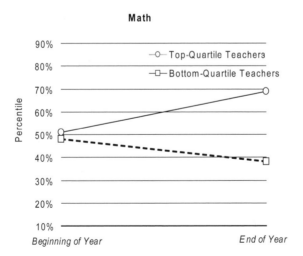

Effective Versus Ineffective Teachers: Studies Involving Secondary Level Students

In a study using data from the Chicago public high schools, the research team estimated the importance of teachers on student mathematics test score gains and then related the measures of individual teacher effectiveness to observable characteristics of the instructors. The study matched student–teacher data for all students enrolled and teachers working in eighty-eight Chicago high schools from 1996–97 to 1998–99; the study concentrated on ninth grade. In the study, teacher quality was defined as the effect on ninth-grade math scores of a semester of instruction with a given teacher, while controlling for eighth-grade math scores and student characteristics. The study revealed the following findings relative to effective versus ineffective teachers (Aaronson, Barrow, & Sander, 2007):

♦ A standard deviation increase in teacher effectiveness over a full year raises student math test scores by 0.15 standard deviations.

♦ Controlling for sampling error, a one standard deviation, one semester improvement in math teacher quality raises student math scores by 0.13 grade equivalents. Thus, over two semesters, a one standard deviation improvement in math teacher quality translates into an increase in math achievement equal to 22 percent of the average annual gain (p. 97).

How Much of the Variability in Student Achievement Can Be Explained by Teacher Effectiveness?

One universal truth that any teacher knows is that students learn differently and at different rates with different results. If two students are in a class, undoubtedly, they will be different in some noted ways in their learning patterns. Why? And what factors lead to these different student learning results?

Obviously, there are many factors that impact how and why students learn as they do: student ability and motivation, home environment and family support, economic conditions, health, school support and prior learning experiences, and so forth. Some of the factors we know and can quantify; others virtually defy quantification, and still others we may not be able even to identify. However, one of the obvious factors that impacts student learning is the quality of teaching. Indeed, the power and importance of the teacher is the central focus of this text.

Estimates of Teacher Effects

Various studies have estimated how much of the variability of student achievement can be explained by the quality of the teacher. In educational research, "variability" has the same meaning as it has in everyday language. To say that student achievement is variable means that it is not the same across individual students. Variability provides a quantitative measure of the degree to which the academic achievement differs among students. Figure 2.6 summarizes selected research regarding how much variability in student achievement can be attributed to the effectiveness of the teacher:

Figure 2.6. Student Achievement Accounted for by Teacher Effects

Study	Approximate Variability in Student Achievement Explained by Teacher Effectiveness
Goldhaber (2002)	8.5 percent
Heistad (1999)	9.2 percent
Nye, Konstantopoulos, & Hedges (2004)	7–21 percent
Rivkin, Hanushek, & Kain (2005)	15 percent
Munoz & Chang (2007)	14 percent

Estimating Teacher Effects Is Not Exact

The empirical studies have been somewhat inconsistent in their findings regarding the magnitude of teacher effects, perhaps as a result of the different methodologies and statistical models they have implemented. Nonetheless, virtually all of the studies do find substantial teacher effects.

In a study exploring the use of large-scale databases in measuring teacher effects on student achievement, Rowan, Correnti, and Miller (2002) calculated a far more robust estimate of classroom (i.e., the teacher) influence on student learning than the findings reporting in Figure 2.6 above. In one analysis using a statistical model[1] they reported as being relatively more valid and reliable than others they experimented with, the authors noted:

> After controlling for student background variables, the classroom to which students were assigned in a given year accounted for roughly *60–61%* of the reliable variance in students' rates of academic growth in reading

1 The authors referred to this analysis as "Model 4: A three-level, cross-classified, random effects model using student gain scores developed by the authors for the study."

achievement and *50–72%* of the reliable variance in students' rates of academic growth in mathematics achievement. This yields…effect sizes ranging from .77–.78 for reading growth, and .72–.85 for mathematics growth. (p. 1532; emphasis added)

The research team stated that these effects are not only statistically significant but also substantively important. The findings of this model suggest that "…holding other conditions constant, a classroom 1 SD higher than another would produce about 2.13 months of added mathematics growth for a student during a calendar year" (p. 1532). In arriving at these findings, they offered some important caveats:

♦ The findings of this model also indicated that classroom effects had only a moderate degree of consistency across difference areas (i.e., reading and mathematics in this case), with correlations ranging from 0.30 to 0.47. This means that "a given teacher varies in effectiveness when teaching different academic subjects" (or even different content areas within the same subject) (p. 1533).

♦ The classroom effects also were influenced by different groups of pupils. Background variables (i.e., socioeconomic status, gender, and minority status in this study) had different effects on annual gains in achievement across classrooms, with these random effects being larger in lower grades (especially in reading) than in upper grades (p. 1533).

Obviously, estimating the influence of teachers (or any variable, for that matter) on student achievement is not a fine science. Indeed, these figures are merely estimates based on the best evidence and statistical measures we have to quantify achievement. Regardless of the studies reviewed, however, what is clear is that teachers are quite influential to student learning.

What Are Practical Implications of Teacher Effects on Student Achievement?

Overall Effects of Teacher Quality on Student Achievement

A large part of the variance in student academic achievement and their achievement gains is derived from the teachers to which they are assigned. The heterogeneity of teacher effectiveness also explains a substantial portion of the between-school variance in student learning. A study by Muijs and Reynolds (2003) found that while controlling for prior student achievement, the effect of teacher behavior is the most significant factor in explaining student progress, explaining 5.6 percent of total variance, and more than 50 percent of the between-classroom variance in student progress over two years.

To further understand the practical significance of effective teachers, the researchers examined the achievement of two students who were taught by the least and the most effective teachers for two years, with all other identifiable factors being comparable between these students. The findings revealed that, after controlling for prior achievement and other confounding variables, the difference on achievement between these two students would be 20 percent, which was totally attributed to variance of effectiveness in the teachers who taught them (Muijs & Reynolds, 2003).

In a study exploring the relative proportion of student achievement gains that can be attributed to each of three general sources—(1) individual differences in student background, (2) classroom effects (including teacher effects), and (3) school effects—the authors found that "teachers have a substantial impact on student learning" (Palardy & Rumberger, 2008, p. 127). In fact, as noted in Chapter 1, teacher effects far outweigh other school effects on student achievement.

In a Tennessee study of primary-grade teachers, the teacher effect size was 0.30 on reading and 0.25 on math, after controlling for student characteristics and classroom composition. "Although these effect sizes would be classified as small by conventional standards, they are substantial in comparison to other factors estimated in this article and to intervention effects estimated elsewhere. For example, the teacher quality effect size for math is approximately 5 times greater than the effect of family [socioeconomic status] found in this study and more than 2.5 times greater than the effect a class-size reduction from 25 to 15 students per classroom" (Palardy & Rumberger, 2008, p. 123). In practical terms, teacher effect sizes convert to:

◆ more than a third (0.38) of a school year of reading achievement gains, and

◆ one-third (0.33) of a school year for math achievement gains. (p. 127)

Importance of Investing in Teacher Quality

School systems devote the overwhelming majority of their resources to teachers and other instructional personnel. "Nevertheless, there is considerable anxiety about teacher quality in American schools today. Not enough highly able people are going into teaching, and too many teachers leave the profession after a few years" (Rothman, 2008, p. 1). Given the undeniable influence of teachers on student success, one clear and compelling practical implication of teacher quality is that we must invest in human capital—that is attracting, developing, supporting, and retaining the best quality teachers possible—in order to help our students experience the success they deserve. Emphasizing this point, Rockoff (2004) concluded from the empirical evidence of his panel data study that "raising teacher quality may be a key instrument in improving student outcomes" (p. 251).

The research findings regarding the magnitude of teacher effects being larger than schools effects[2] sheds light on the policy issue of educational resource allocation. Because the classroom teacher is a larger source of variance in student achievement than the school, policies focusing on teacher effects should be more promising than policies tinkering with school effects. Many school-level policies that attempt to improve achievement by substituting one school for another (e.g., school choice, charter school) or changing the structure of the schools themselves (e.g., whole-school reform; reform on curriculum standards) have turned out to be disappointing (Barber & Mourshed, 2007; Nye, Konstantopoulos, & Hedges, 2004). As an example of the power of investing in teachers, some high-performing East Asian countries found that mechanisms to encourage high levels of student achievement include ongoing professional development and the equalization of instructional resources—policies targeting classroom teachers (Akiba, LeTendre, & Scribner, 2007).

Human Capital Applied to Education

So, what is human capital? In the private sector, human capital is generally defined as the accumulated value of an individual's intellect, knowledge, experience, competencies, and commitment that contributes to the achievement of an organization's vision and business objectives….When we apply this idea to K-12 education, we realize that our "business objective," or bottom line, is student achievement. In public education, human capital refers to the knowledge and skill sets of our teachers that directly result in increased levels of learning for students. In short, we are talking about what teachers know and are able to do—their talent level. (Sigler & Kashyap, 2008, p. 1)

How Can Teacher Effects Help with Equity for All Students?

Research indicates that in American public school systems, effective teachers are among the most inequitably distributed resources we have (Si-

---

2 More details on this topic are reported in Chapter 1.

gler & Kashyap, 2008). Unfortunately, too many teachers lack the knowledge and skills they need to teach all students effectively.

> Year after year, decade after decade, countless studies told us that on these measures, we didn't have a fair distribution of teacher talent.... Recently, the state education department in Tennessee took a close look at what these data told them about the kinds of students being taught by the strongest—and weakest—teachers in the state. Unfortunately, what they found echoes the pattern in the proxy data: Poor children and black children were less likely to be taught by the strongest teachers and more likely to be taught by the weakest. (Gordon, Kane, & Staiger, 2006, pp. 15–16)

Equity and Teacher Quality

"And the students who need the strongest instruction often are taught by teachers with the least experience and expertise." (Rothman, 2008, p.1)

An important finding in Nye, Konstantopoulos, and Hedges' (2004) study of primary-grade teachers in Tennessee is that the between-teacher (but within-school and within-treatment) variance is always larger in low socioeconomic status schools. This finding suggests that the distribution of teacher effectiveness is much more uneven in low socioeconomic status schools than in high socioeconomic status schools. Additionally, the proportion of the total variance in student achievement gains accounted for by the teacher effect is higher in low socioeconomic status schools. Thus, it matters more which teacher a child receives in low socioeconomic status schools than it does in high socioeconomic status schools.

A major value-added teacher effectiveness study by Bembry, Jordan, Gomez, Anderson, and Mendro (1998) found through a bias analysis of the data that students with low achievement tend to be assigned to less effective teachers and students with high achievement tend to be assigned to more effective teachers. Additionally, the study discovered that uneven distribution of quality teachers is not a random or occasional occurrence, but a systemic bias.

As Bembry et al. (1998), noted, these findings suggest very practical implications regarding equitable opportunities for all students. In particular, consider the following related findings:

♦ All students deserve quality education, but equal access to quality education is jeopardized for students who are assigned to a less effective teacher.

- It is the school's responsibility to remediate students who are already affected by less-than-effective teachers (Bembry, et. al., 1998).

- For all students of all achievement levels, teacher assignment sequences should be determined in a manner to ensure that no student is assigned to a teacher sequence (high effectiveness versus low effectiveness teachers) that will unduly diminish the student's academic achievement (Sanders & Rivers, 1996).

- School policy on teacher quality can be an important tool for raising the achievement of low income students. In particular, successive assignment of good teachers can be a big step toward closing achievement gaps across income groups (Rivkin, Hanushek, & Kain, 2005). Based on the teacher effects estimates by Gordon, Kane, and Staiger (2006), the average achievement difference between being assigned to a top-quartile teacher and a bottom-quartile teacher is 10 percentile points. Currently, the national black–white achievement gap in the United States is around 30 percentile points. Because the teacher impact is cumulative, having a top-quartile teacher for three to four years in a row would help substantially in closing the achievement gap.

Conclusion

It seems quite clear that the quality of teaching is the most important school-related factor in student achievement (see, e.g., Education Trust, 2001; Rothman, 2008; Sigler & Kashyap, 2008). Consequently, without effective teachers neither our schools as a whole, nor our students individually and collectively, can experience the gains and improvement we desire.

3

Why Do Teachers Matter?

Teacher effects on student achievement have been found to be both additive and cumulative with little evidence that subsequent effective teachers can offset the effects of ineffective ones.

— Sanders & Horn (1997, p. 247)

Why does it matter so much that we have teachers who are as effective as possible teaching our students year after year? After all, spending a year with a less-than-effective teacher will be over soon enough and the child can move on. Not so.

When those pesky parents ask us to assign *their* children to a particular teachers' classroom, what do we say? "Oh, don't worry. Your child will learn what she needs to learn from *any* teacher in our school." Well, that turns out to be a lie. (Haycock & Crawford, 2008, p. 14)

This chapter addresses matters related to the enduring impact of teachers on students' lives. In particular, key questions related to teachers' lasting effect are addressed:

- ♦ How do cumulative effects of teachers impact student achievement?

- ♦ How do residual effects of teachers impact student achievement?

- ♦ What are the implications of teacher quality for selected student populations?

How Do Cumulative Effects of Teachers Impact Student Achievement?

What Is Cumulative Effect?

Generally speaking, *cumulative effect* refers to the additive influence that a variable can have on a subject if that subject is exposed to the influencing variable repeatedly. For example, take the application of cumulative effect applied to repeated doses of a given medicine as indicated in the following medical definition:

cumulative effect cu·mu·la·tive ef·fect

n. The state at which repeated administration of a drug may produce effects that are more pronounced than those produced by the first dose. ("cumulative effect," 2009)

In practical terms *cumulative effect* means that the "effects...resulting from actions that are individually minor...add up to a greater total effect as they take place over a period of time" ("cumulative effects," 2009). Thus, cumulative effects are additive.

In education circles, *cumulative effect* considers the additive influence of teachers, year after year, on student gains. Applying cumulative effects to the Tennessee Value-Added Assessment System (TVAAS), the researchers considered "the cumulative average gain [to be] the primary indicator by which success is measured," thus, making growth the consistent focus of analysis (Sanders, Saxton, & Horn, 1997, p. 139). And when we consider the impact of a series of teachers on student learning, across twelve or thirteen years of elementary and secondary education, we have a picture of the cumulative influence of teachers on student achievement.

Student gain scores and cumulative effects of teachers appear to be impervious to typical factors associated with measures of student achievement, such as race, ethnicity, and socioeconomic level. Sanders and Horn (1998), in analyzing the cumulative gains for schools across the State of Tennessee "found them to be unrelated to the racial composition of schools, the percentage of students receiving free and reduced-price lunches, or the mean achievement level of the school" (p. 251). Thus, factors that are often associated with low achievement levels in absolute terms, such as race and poverty, are not associated with achievement gains. "According to one observer, TVAAS has helped to shift the focus from absolute achievement levels to learning gains and has, thereby, helped to identify some real heroes in the Tennessee schools who have been overlooked in the past despite the notable learning gains they have made with students" (Tucker & Stronge, 2005, p. 77).

Using the Tennessee Comprehensive Assessment Program data, the following basic steps are taken to make the testing information useful to teachers, administrators, and educational policy makers:

1. Determine the *improvement* or gain in test scores for each subject for each student;

2. Compare each student's *actual* gain to the *expected* gain based on the student's past performance;

3. Compile individual student gains at the class, school, district, and state levels; and

4. Compare aggregated data to average gains for the school, district, state, and nation.

Applying Cumulative Effects

Sanders and Rivers (1996) found that teacher effects on student learning are cumulative. For example, the average fifth-grade student who had been assigned to highly effective teachers three years in a row will score a mean of 50 percentile points higher in mathematics than peers who have had ineffective teachers three years in a row. Subsequent analyses of the TVSSA longitudinal student achievement data revealed interesting findings:

♦ Cumulative gains in student achievement are unrelated to the racial composition of schools or the percentage of students receiving free and reduced-price lunches (Sanders & Horns, 1998).

♦ Students at the highest level of achievement are making less academic gains than lower-achieving students in a large percentage of Tennessee schools, especially those located in the metropolitan areas (Sanders & Horn, 1997).

In a value-added study of students in Los Angeles, students taught by teachers in the top quartile of effectiveness advanced, on average, approximately 5 percentile points each year relative to their peers, whereas those taught by teachers in the bottom quartile of effectiveness lost, on average, 5 percentile points relative to their peers (Gordon, Kane, & Staiger, 2006, as cited in Haycock & Crawford, 2008). "Moreover, these effects are *cumulative*" (Haycock & Crawford, 2008, p. 15 [*emphasis added*]).

Cumulative Effect Illustrated

A good example of cumulative effect can be drawn from the Dallas, Texas, Public Schools. After collecting value-added student achievement data over several years, a team in their research department asked a provocative question: What would happen if a child were placed in highly effective teachers' classes three years in a row, beginning in grade 2? Conversely, what would happen if that child were placed in three ineffective teachers' classes three years running? The results of this post-hoc study are summarized in Figures 3.1 (for reading achievement) and 3.2 (for math achievement) (Jordan, Mendro, & Weerasinghe, 1997).

Figure 3.1. Cumulative Effect on Reading Achievement from 3 Years Instruction with Highly Effective vs. Ineffective Teachers: 2nd–4th Grades

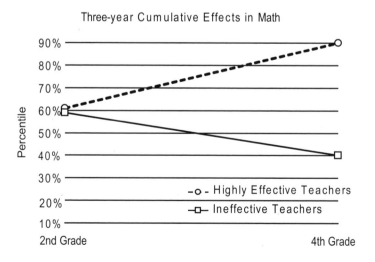

Three-year Cumulative Effects in Reading

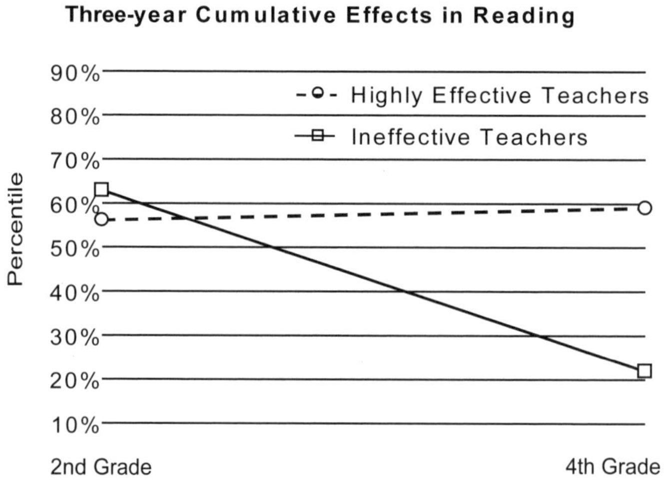

Figure 3.2. Cumulative Effect on Math Achievement from 3 Years Instruction with Highly Effective vs. Ineffective Teachers: 2nd–4th Grades

Three-year Cumulative Effects in Math

Drawing on these and other value-added findings, an overlapping team of researchers from the Dallas Public Schools surmised that teachers have significant effects on student achievement, and those effects (either positive or negative) are strongly *accumulative* over time (Bembry, Jordan, Gomez, Anderson, & Mendro, 1998). Consequently, teachers are far more influential in the success (or failure) of students than we might initially realize. The influence under the tutelage of a teacher—effective or otherwise—lasts far longer than merely a given school year. Moreover, the child will build on those learning experiences in subsequent years.

Similar results regarding teachers' cumulative effects were found in a value-added study in England. Barber and Mourshed (2007) found that "the negative impact of low-performing teachers is severe, particularly during the earlier years of schooling. At the primary level, students that are placed with low-performing teachers for several years in a row suffer an educational loss which is largely irreversible" (p. 12). In England, by age seven, children who score in the top 20 percent on tests of numeracy and literacy are already twice as likely to complete a university degree as children in the bottom 20 percent. Additionally, students that fail at age 11 have only a 25 percent chance of meeting the grade standard at age 14. And for the students who fail at age 14, the chance to graduate with the expected minimum set of school-leaving qualifications falls to just 6 percent. The stern facts from England indicate that both teacher impact and student academic achievement are accumulative. Consequently, without the intervention of effective teachers in the classroom, students are most likely to be caught in a vicious cycle of failure.

Cumulative Effect and Socioeconomic Influences

No doubt, innate dispositions and capacity influence how much and how well all of us learn and achieve. Nonetheless, to a large degree, all learners are products of their environment—school, community, and home. Consider the preschool learning opportunities provided for children as an artifact of socioeconomic status presented in Figure 3.3.

Figure 3.3. Influence of Socioeconomic Status Home Environment on Vocabulary Development of Preschool Children

	Words Spoken to Per Hour	Vocabulary at 5 Years Old
Children whose parents hold professional jobs	2,100	20,000
Children from low socioeconomic backgrounds	600	5,000

Moreover, consider the entry level skill disparities of kindergarten children from high and low socioeconomic backgrounds (Figure 3.4).

Figure 3.4. Beginning Kindergartners' School-Readiness Skills Based on Socioeconomic Status

	Lowest Socioeconomic Status	Highest Socioeconomic Status
Recognizes letters of the alphabet	39%	85%
Identifies beginning sounds of words	10%	51%
Identifies primary colors	69%	90%
Counts to 20	48%	68%
Writes own name	54%	76%
Amount of time read to prior to kindergarten	25 hours	1,000 hours

Sources: Lee & Burkam, 2002; West, Denton, & Germino-Hausken, 2000

What is clear from these summary data is that children do not enter school equally prepared to learn. Some children have been advantaged with enriching learning experiences; other children have not. Moreover, these findings make clear how important all learning opportunities—formal and informal, home and school—are to the cumulative achievement of children. This is the essence of cumulative effect: Children aren't born at the 90th percentile;

instead, they arrive there over time as a result of their cumulative learning experiences.

How Do Residual Effects of Teachers Impact Student Achievement?

What Is Residual Effect?

residual re·sid·u·al

1 : remainder, residuum: as ... b : a residual product or substance c : an internal aftereffect of experience or activity that influences later behavior; especially : a disability remaining from a disease or operation ("residual," 2009)

As suggested in the above definition, residual relates to something left after other parts have been taken away. In other words, *residual effect* refers to the aftereffect of a variable on a subject. For our purposes in discussing value-added assessment, we focus on the residual effects of teachers on student learning. To say that a teacher's effect is residual means that the teacher's impact on students persists even after the students have been pulled out from the teacher's tutelage for one year, two years, or three years.

Available evidence suggests that teacher effects are cumulative with little evidence of compensatory effects of more effective teachers in later grades (Sanders & Horn, 1998). It is a false assumption that assigning a highly effective teacher to students who have had an ineffective teacher can make up the difference.

- The residual effects of both effective and ineffective teachers are measurable two years later, regardless of the effectiveness of subsequent teachers (Sanders & Horn, 1998).

- Even three years of time cannot remedy entirely the loss of achievement (Bembry, Jordan, Gomez, Anderson, & Mendro, 1998).[1]

- Ineffective teachers have negative longitudinal effects on student learning. If the students have a less-effective teacher in the first year and the highest level teachers for remaining years, their achievement could never exceed that of the students who have been assigned with effective teachers for all the years (Mendro, Jordan, Gomez, Anderson, & Bemby, 1998a,b).

---

1 Note that the Bembry, et. al. study found differences three years later, whereas the Sanders and Horn study noted differences two years later.

Residual Effect Illustrated

In their review of the cumulative and residual effects of teachers on student achievement, Sanders and Rivers (1996) detailed the powerful influence of teachers on the future success of students they taught. Groups of students with comparable abilities and initial achievement levels may have vastly different academic outcomes as a result of the sequence of teachers to which they were assigned. In an extreme case comparison, Sanders and Rivers (1996) found that for students who begin second grade (i.e., seven-year-olds) at the same level, there is a stark difference after three years of being assigned to a series of low-low-low teachers versus high-high-high teachers (Figure 3.5).

Figure 3.5. Residual Effects of 3-Year Sequence of High- vs. Low-Effectiveness Teachers

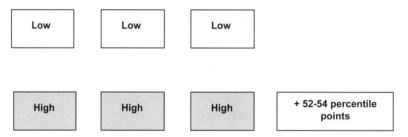

In a less extreme comparison, Sanders and Rivers observed a difference of 13 percentile points between students with a low-low-high sequence of teacher effectives versus those with a high-high-high sequence (Figure 3.6).

Figure 3.6. Residual Effects of 3-Year Sequence of High- vs. Low-Effectiveness Teachers

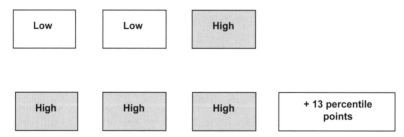

As suggested in Figure 3.6, residual effects of relatively ineffective teachers from prior years could still be measured in subsequent achievement scores, even after the mitigating effect of being assigned to a highly effective teacher in a subsequent year. It is encouraging to note, however, that there is no significant interaction between teachers of different effectiveness levels over various grades. This means that an effective teacher receiving students from a relatively ineffective teacher can still facilitate excellent achievement gains in the students, despite the negative residual effects (Sanders & Rivers, 1996). With three years of effective teachers, at least students have a 1 in 8 chance of making it back to the top (Mendro, Jordan, Gomez, Anderson, & Bemby, 1998a,b).

The Power of Teachers' Residual Effects

Being assigned to a highly effective teacher is like an investment that pays dividends for years to come; unfortunately, being assigned to an ineffective teacher is like paying a penalty year after year.

What Are the Implications of Teacher Effectiveness for Selected Student Populations?

Clearly, the carryover effect of teacher effectiveness has significant implications for student success. The residual influence of effective and ineffective teachers touches the lives of all learners. At the same time, extant research is yielding valuable lessons regarding how the residual effect phenomenon influences the success (or failure) of various student groups. Consider the following findings related to specified student subpopulations:

Teacher Effectiveness and Minority Students

♦ "African-American students and white students make comparable academic progress when they are assigned to teachers of comparable effectiveness. However, at least in the system studied (Tennessee), black students were disproportionately assigned to the least effective teachers. The cumulative effects of such a pattern of assignment of students to teachers, offers at least a partial explanation for the widening gap between the mean achievement test scores of black and white student populations" (Sanders & Horn, 1997, p. 3).

- In a study of Chicago public high schools, estimates of teacher effects varied by initial (eighth grade) test scores, race, and sex. The biggest impact of a higher quality teacher, relative to the mean gain of that group, was among African American students. There was no difference between boys and girls (Aaronson, Barrow, & Sander, 2007, p. 97).

- A one standard deviation, one semester increase in teacher quality raises ninth-grade test score performance by 0.20 grade equivalents (23 percent of the average annual gain) for African American students and 0.13 grade equivalents (11 percent of the average annual gain) for Hispanic students. The difference in less important for non-African American, non-Hispanic students (Aaronson, Barrow, & Sander, 2007).

- Drawing from a Los Angeles study, "…if all black students were assigned to four highly effective teachers in a row, this would be sufficient to close the average black–white achievement gap" (Haycock & Crawford, 2008, p. 15).

Teacher Effectiveness and High Ability Students

- As the level of teacher effectiveness increases, lower-achieving students were first to benefit, followed by average students, and, lastly, by students considerably above average. Only the most effective teachers achieved excellent academic progress with the highest-performing students (Sanders & Horn, 1998).

  "There is a disturbingly common but not universal pattern for the best students to make the lowest gains" (Wright, Horn, & Sanders, 1997, p. 65). "Possible explanations include lack of opportunity for high-scoring students to proceed at their own pace, lack of challenging materials, lack of accelerated course offering, and concentration of instruction on the average or below-average student" (Wright, Horn, & Sanders, 1997, p. 66). (Note: Another possible contributing factor could be the statistical problem of "ceiling effect" with student scores.)

- Through systematic observations in elementary-level regular classrooms, one research team found that there was no curricular or instructional differentiation provided for high-ability students in 84 percent of learning activities (Westberg, Archambault, Dobyns, & Salvin, 1993).

- Compared with high-ability learners, low-achieving students are more likely to be the top priority of teachers. On a national survey of 900 teachers in grades 2 through 12 conducted by the Fordham Institute, 81 percent of the teachers stated that they tend to give one-on-one attention to academically struggling students, but only 5 percent give such attention to advanced students (Duffet, Farkas, & Loveless, 2008).

♦ National Assessment of Educational Progress (NAEP) scores for U.S. students indicate that lowest-achieving students have made solid and rapid gains from 2000 to 2007, whereas the performance of highest-achieving students was stagnant (Duffet, Farkas, & Loveless, 2008).

Teacher Effectiveness and Economically Disadvantaged Students

♦ Economically disadvantaged students systematically achieve less than their more advantaged peers, on average 0.6 standard deviations each year (Rivkin, Hanushek, & Kain, 2005).

♦ An effective teacher is effective with all students, regardless of their socioeconomic status background; conversely, an ineffective teacher is ineffective with all students (Nye, Konstantopoulos, & Hedges, 2004).

♦ Among 39 countries, the United States ranked 36th in its ability to provide equal access to qualified math teachers for low and high socioeconomic status students. In fact, 67.6 percent of high socioeconomic status students were taught by high qualification teachers compared with 53.2 percent for low socioeconomic status students, showing the opportunity gap of 14.4 percent which is significantly larger than the international average of 2.5 percent (Akiba, LeTendre, & Scribner, 2007).

♦ Low income and minority students face higher teacher turnover and tend to be taught more frequently by beginning teachers (Rivkin, Hanushek, & Kain, 2005, p. 450).

♦ The estimated variation in the quality of instruction reveals that schools and teachers play an important role in promoting economic and social equity. A poor child who has high-quality teachers for five consecutive years could have large enough learning gains to close the achievement gap with their upper-income peers and offset the disadvantage associated with low socioeconomic background (Rivkin, Hanushek, & Kain, 2005).

Conclusion: So Why Do Teachers Matter?

In their study of eighty-eight Chicago public high schools, Aaronson, Barrow, and Sander (2007) estimated the importance of teachers on student mathematics test score gains and then related the student achievement measures to individual teacher effectiveness.[2] In this study, the measure of teacher quality was defined as the effect on ninth-grade math scores of a semester of instruction with a given teacher, while controlling for eighth-grade math scores and student characteristics. The findings revealed that the dispersion of teacher quality is wide and educationally significant.

> Controlling for sampling error, a one standard deviation, one semester improvement in math teacher quality raises student math scores by 0.13 grade equivalents. Thus, over two semesters, a one standard deviation improvement in math teacher quality translates into an increase in math achievement equal to 22 percent of the average annual gain. (Aaronson, Barrow, and Sander, 2007, p. 97)

Economists Rivkin, Hanushek, and Kain (2005) reached a similar conclusion. A substantial share of the overall achievement gain variation occurs between teachers. Moreover, they surmised that teachers have powerful effects on reading and mathematics achievement. Additionally, much of the teacher quality variation exists within rather than between schools.

- A one standard deviation increase in average teacher quality for a grade raises average student achievement in the grade by at least 0.11 standard deviation of the total test score distribution in *mathematics*.

- A one standard deviation increase in average teacher quality for a grade raises average student achievement in the grade by 0.095 standard deviation in *reading*. (p. 434)

Given the findings from the various studies cited in this chapter, it is apparent that teachers have a dramatic impact on student success—not only now, but also for years to come, which is why the quality of our teachers matters so significantly.

---

2 The study concentrated on ninth grade teachers and students.

4

How Do Teachers Matter?[1]

From Aristotle and Socrates to Montessori and Piaget to Bruner and Hanushek, philosophers, physicians, psychologists, cognitive scientists, and economists have each attempted to characterize the attributes, dispositions, knowledge, and instructional skills that define effective teachers. The rationale for this 2000-year search is that better teachers produce better learning.

— Schacter & Thum (2004, p. 411)

The focus of the book to this point has been on how much teachers impact student achievement, the lasting effects of teachers' impact on student learning, and why teacher quality matters. However, it simply isn't enough to determine how much teachers matter; we must determine what teachers do that matters so inordinately. In this chapter, the overarching issue is: What are the background qualities, dispositions, skills, and behaviors that, in fact, do make a difference in student achievement? As factors of teacher quality are explored in depth, the following guiding questions are addressed:

- ◆ Why should we care about what makes a teacher effective?
- ◆ What is a framework for understanding effective teachers' qualities and dispositions?
- ◆ How do teachers' background qualities affect student achievement?

---

1 This chapter was coauthored by Xianxuan Xu.

- How do teachers' skills and practices affect student achievement?

- So what makes good teachers good? Putting the evidence together.

Why Should We Care about What Makes a Teacher Effective?

Student learning is the professional touchstone for any educational program and teacher. The purpose of teaching is to nurture learning, and both teachers and school should be judged for their effectiveness on the basis of what and how much students learn (Schalock, Schalock, Cowart, & Myton, 1993). The social contract between public education and society requires schools to hire, retain, and improve teachers who have the qualities that are most predictive of student achievement. A greater understanding of what constitutes teacher effects has significant implications for the decision making regarding recruitment, compensation, training, and evaluation of teachers. If we hire effective or, at least, promising, teachers, we will have better teachers for the duration of their service, which is why the role of human resources is so critical to teacher quality and students' opportunity to learn.

Considering the human capital and physical capital invested, teaching is one of the biggest professions, and education is one of the largest industries. In 2002 alone, the United States invested $192 billion in teacher pay and benefits (Rice, 2003). Additionally, billions of dollars are spent each year on teacher professional development, bailouts of ineffective teachers, high rate of teacher turnovers, and so on. Considering the size of such a cost, remarkably little is known about what qualities make an effective teacher and what constitutes effective teaching. Without a strong and solid foundation of educational research, the critical decisions regarding who to hire, who to retain, and what to include in teacher professional development could only be made on the quick sands of untested intuition and experience.

Inquiry into Teacher Effectiveness

The inquiry into what makes a teacher effective can lead to better educated societies that not only increase the quality of life of people that participated in them, but create many economic, cultural, and civic advances. (Schacter & Thum, 2004, p. 411)

It is well established that teachers vary in their ability to improve student achievement; however, there is a lot to learn regarding what explains this heterogeneity in teacher quality. The extant research on teacher dispositions, qualifications, experience, and instructional skills has not found a silver-bullet teacher characteristic that can explain student learning. If we are to move beyond merely identifying the impact of effective (and ineffective) teachers on student learning, it is essential that we go inside the classroom and figure out how these highly effective teachers are teaching. What are they doing differently? How are they engaging students? Why do students work so hard for them? How do they sustain—day after day and year after year—a focus on what matters most for student success?

If we are to understand how teachers impact student learning, we must open the black box of the classroom and peer inside. As one research team reported in *Teachers College Record*:

> The time has come to move beyond variance decomposition models that estimate the random effects of schools and classrooms on student achievement. These analyses *treat the classroom as a black box*, and although they can be useful in identifying more and less effective classrooms, and in telling us how much of a natural variation in classroom effectiveness can make to student achievement, variance decomposition models do not tell us why some classrooms are more effective than others…we would argue that future large-scale research on teaching move to directly measuring instructional conditions inside classrooms, assessing the implementation and effectiveness of deliberately designed instructional interventions, or both. (Rowan, Correnti, & Miller, 2002, pp. 1554–1555, *emphasis added*)

What Is a Framework for Understanding Effective Teachers Qualities and Dispositions?

What Effective Teachers Do that Impacts Student Achievement

Dan Goldhaber, a well-respected researcher on matters related to teacher quality posed a question that reaches to the core of what this chapter addresses:

> What does the empirical evidence have to say about specific characteristics of teachers and their relationship to student achievement? (2002, p. 3)

In responding to this fundamental question, Goldhaber noted a number of cautions regarding connecting teacher qualities to student achievement:

> It is important to note that studies focus on different grade levels, subjects, and types of students taught, and in some cases the estimated effects

of particular attributes are not consistent across the board. Furthermore, studies vary considerably in quality. Experiments, which provide the most credible results, are rare in education, and relatively few studies that address students' outcomes observe the professional norm of having detailed controls for students' background characteristics (including previous academic achievement). (2002, p. 3)

Nonetheless, he offered a broad overview of the findings for various teacher attributes, including:

♦ *Teacher degree and experience levels:* Teachers' degree and experience levels are widely studied teacher attributes. One reason is that data of these characteristics can be easily collected. The other reason is that these two attributes are the sole determinants of teachers' salaries in most school systems and they are subject to the influence of education policy. Consequently, policy makers and educators are especially interested in examining how they are correlated to teacher effectiveness. However, there is not strong evidence from research showing that these characteristics consistently and positively influence student learning. In fact, teachers' degree and experience seem to matter only in certain circumstances.

♦ *Subject-matter knowledge:* Research generally used degree, coursework, and certification status to measure a teacher's knowledge of subject matter. The findings are mixed. It seems that for math and science, the academic preparation of teachers has a positive impact on student achievement. Additionally, students of higher grades achieve more when their teachers have greater knowledge of subject matter.

♦ *Teachers' pedagogical knowledge:* There is little research directly assessing the influence of pedagogical training on student outcomes. Existing research has focused on the impact of teachers' performance on licensure exams and the merits of licensing teachers. Unfortunately, there is little evidence of a large and consistent association between teacher certification and student achievement. Some studies found that the effects of certification are small and specific to certain contexts.

♦ *Other teacher attributes:* There were studies examining the effects of other measurable attributes such as teachers' academic scores on SAT or ACT, verbal ability, or the selectivity of the undergraduate institution. However, the estimated magnitudes of these attributes are relatively weak.

A Framework for Teacher Quality

In *Qualities of Effective Teachers* (Stronge, 2007), I presented a framework for six teacher qualities based on a meta-review of the extant research on teacher effectiveness[2] that largely matches the descriptions noted above.

- *Prerequisites for Effective Teaching*, including characteristics such as a teacher's educational background, professional preparation, verbal ability, content knowledge, educational coursework, and teacher certification.

- *Teacher Dispositions*, with an emphasis on a teacher's nonacademic interactions with students and professional attitude.

- *Classroom Management*, with the purpose of establishing a classroom environment that is conducive to teaching and learning.

- *Planning for Instruction*, including the practices of maximizing the amount of time allocated for instruction, communicating expectations for student achievement, and planning for instructional purposes.

- *Implementing Instruction*, including the practices of using instructional strategies according to particulars of students needs, understanding the complexities of teaching, using questioning techniques and supporting student engagement.

- *Assessing Student Progress*, such as using homework and ongoing assessment to solicit data of student learning, providing meaningful feedback, and applying the findings of student learning outcomes to improve instruction.

An adaptation of these qualities is summarized in Figure 4.1. The two major categories below—*teacher background qualities* and *teacher skills and practices*—will serve as the organizing framework for presenting a summary of what we know about the connection between teacher qualities and student achievement.

---

2 For a comprehensive analysis and discussion of the qualities of effective teachers, along with selected tools to apply the qualities in instructional practice and supervision, see Stronge (2007).

Figure 4.1. A Framework for Teacher Effectiveness

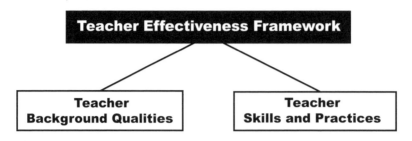

How Do Teachers' Background Qualities Affect Student Achievement?

Variability in Research on Background Characteristics

How do teachers' background qualities affect student achievement? Several research streams from the areas of education and economics provide some exploratory answers to this question. The background characteristics that have been examined in the research literature include degrees, coursework, certification status, experience, verbal skills, subject-matter knowledge, academic achievement, and the prestige ratings of teachers' undergraduate institutions. However the research literature has not produced consistent findings and no consensus has been reached regarding what aspects of teachers matter most. For instance, certain studies have found that teacher background characteristics are positively associated with student achievement; others have found they are negatively related; and still others have found they are positively associated only in certain specific circumstances.

In an extensive literature review, Hahushek (1997) synthesized the education production function research on the association between school resources and student achievement. He found that the data assembled did not provide evidence of a strong and consistent relation between teacher characteristics (as a form of school resource) and student learning. On the other hand, a review conducted by Greenwald, Hedges, and Laine (1996) found that the relationship between school resource inputs and student outcomes are much more consistent and positive. In this study, resource variables that capture the quality of teachers—such as teacher ability, teacher education, and teacher experience—showed strong relationships with student achievement.

A review by Wayne and Youngs (2003) applied a set of study design criteria on the pool of studies that treated student achievement. After the screening, only 21 studies were included in the final review, with each having controlled for students' prior achievement and socioeconomic status. They found evidence that the ratings of undergraduate institutions and test scores (on teacher licensure examinations and verbal ability tests) had consistently positive associations with student achievement gains. However, the findings on effects of degrees, coursework, and certification were inconclusive. Nonetheless, these three characteristics (degrees, coursework, and certification) were found to be positively related to achievement for specific subject areas and grades—specifically, high school mathematics, where high school students learn more from teachers with certification in mathematics, mathematics-related degrees, and mathematics-related college-level coursework.

Despite the variability in research regarding teacher background characteristics and student achievement, there are a number of well-supported findings that should be considered, especially teacher background factors that serve as inputs at the classroom level for the process of interaction between teachers and students. Additionally, these background qualities correlate with "presage variables," a term used by Rowan, Correnti, and Miller (2002), which they defined as "properties of teachers that can be assumed to operate prior to, but also to have an influence on, the interactive phase of teaching" (p. 1538). Selected teacher background qualities and their relationship to student achievement will be explored in turn.

Teacher Background Qualities: A Priori Factors
Degrees Earned

Degree level and area of degree attained by the teacher have been a widely examined characteristic in quantitative studies. Generally, the research is inconclusive as to how degrees contribute to student achievement. Several studies found no statistically significant effect of teacher degree level on teacher effectiveness as measured by student achievement gains, while controlling for confounding effects of student background and other teacher-related characteristics (Hanushek, Kain, & Rivkin, 1998; Munoz & Chang, 2007; Rivkin, Hanushek, & Kain, 2005).

Hanushek, Kain, and Rivkin (1998) analyzed a large sample of student achievement data in Texas and used value-added regression to disentangle the separate factors influencing achievement. This study identified the impact of specific, measured components of teachers and schools on achievement. The study revealed that there was no evidence that postgraduate education can improve the quality of teaching. Actually, the estimates for the effects of a master's degree were generally negative and always statistically insignificant. A more recent study conducted by the same research team (Rivkin, Hanushek, & Kain, 2005) used an extraordinarily rich database of more than 600,000 students in mathematics and reading and spanning grades 3 through

7. This study also found that teacher quality cannot be attributed to observable characteristics like teacher education level: There was no evidence that a master's degree raises teacher effectiveness. Another value-added study conducted by Munoz and Chang (2007) reached a similar conclusion: Teacher educational level did not add to the prediction in students' growth rates of achievement; in other words, teacher education was not significantly related to their students' growth rates.

Elementary School Teacher Degree Attainment and Student Achievement

Rowan, Correnti, and Miller (2002) used a large-scale student achievement database on reading and math from grade 1 through grade 6, drawn from *Prospects: The Congressionally Mandated Study of Educational Growth and Opportunity 1991–1994*. This study used three-level hierarchical linear modeling to test the effects of teacher attributes on student achievement. The researchers found that in elementary grade-level reading, teachers' degree status had statistically significant effects on growth in students' achievement. And in elementary mathematics, students who were taught by a teacher with an advanced degree in mathematics did worse than those who were taught by a teacher not having a mathematics degree. Thus, the evidence regarding the impact of advanced degrees at the elementary level is, to some extent, counterintuitive.

Secondary School Teacher Degree Attainment and Student Achievement

Unlike studies with elementary school teachers, the studies that focused on high school mathematics have been quite consistent in their findings of a positive association between advanced degrees and student achievement. Rowan, Chiang, and Miller (1997) examined student achievement data on eighth grade through tenth grade math, drawn from the longitudinal files of the National Education Longitudinal Study of 1988 (NELS: 88). They found students assigned to teachers who majored in mathematics at the undergraduate and/or graduate level had higher levels of mathematics achievement than those whose teachers did not, although the effect was quite small. Goldhaber and Brewer (1997a, 2000) conducted two studies, both of which found that high school student achievement gains in mathematics were positively related to teachers who hold a bachelor's and/or master's degree in mathematics. Both studies draw on the dataset of *National Educational Longitudinal Study of 1988* (NELS: 88). The study done in 1997 found that tenth-grade mathematics students who were taught by teachers having master's degrees in mathematics had higher achievement gains than those whose teachers had either no advanced degrees or advanced degrees in nonmathematics subjects. This study also found that students whose teachers had bachelor's degrees in mathematics achieved more than students whose teachers had bachelor's degrees in nonmathematics subjects. The study conducted in 2000 found that twelfth-grade mathematics students learn more from teachers with mathematics majors and from teachers with master's degrees in mathematics. Findings regarding the impact of college degree on student achievement are summarized in Figure 4.2.

Figure 4.2. General Findings Regarding Impact of Teachers' College Degree on Student Achievement

School Level	Impact of Advanced Degree on Student Achievement
Elementary School Level	Inconclusive or negative impact
Secondary School Level	Positive impact

Educational Coursework

Another teacher attribute that is closely related with degree is teachers' course taking. Over the last several decades, policy makers and researchers have used measures of the level and type of coursework taken by teachers as proxies for what teachers know and can do in their classrooms.

In a review of the literature on teacher attributes that are linked to student achievement gains, Wayne and Youngs (2003) cited the following two studies that had focused on teacher coursework:

♦ Controlling for student background and other teacher-related characteristics, Eberts and Stone (1984) found no relationship between fourth graders' mathematics achievement and the number of college-level, mathematics-related courses taken by their teachers.

♦ Monk and King (1994) used hierarchical linear modeling to analyze achievement data in mathematics and science, drawn from the *Longitudinal Survey of American Youth* (LSAY). Although the study yielded many indeterminate findings, the relationship between high school mathematics gains and teacher coursework was quite strong. They found tenth and eleventh-grade students made more achievement gains when their mathematics teachers had more mathematics courses.

Another study based on data from the LSAY (Monk, 1994) is often cited in the discussion about the effects of teacher coursework, although it did not control for student background characteristics, LSAY is a panel survey dataset that includes a base-year sample of 2,829 high school students from fifty-one randomly selected public high schools. This study used student achievement scores in mathematics and science of tenth, eleventh, and twelfth grades, and related them to teacher characteristics. Monk found that the number of college-level mathematics or science courses taken by teachers had a positive effect on student learning gains in mathematics and science. The more traditional teacher inputs, such as teacher experience or degree level, proved unrelated to student achievement. Interestingly, the evidence from this study also suggests that effects of subject matter preparation diminish with time and vary across types of students (such as advanced versus remedial); the effect of content coursework levels off after five courses for high school teachers. Monk found that the effects of coursework on pedagogy are more stable over time.

In a synthesis of literature on the association between teacher attributes and student learning, Rice (2003) found coursework in both the subject area taught and pedagogy have a positive impact on student achievement, particularly the impact of subject-specific coursework for high school mathematics. However, in other subjects and grade levels, the impact of teacher content-course-taking on student achievement was found to be indeterminant and inconsistent. In addition, pedagogical coursework contributed to teacher effectiveness at all grade levels, mostly when coupled with content knowledge. Figure 4.3 summarizes the findings regarding the impact of coursework on student achievement.

Figure 4.3. General Findings Regarding Impact of Teachers' Course-taking on Student Achievement

Type of Coursework	Impact on Student Achievement
Content courses (e.g., mathematics)	Positive impact
Pedagogical courses (e.g., how to teach math)	Positive impact

Certification Status

Historically, policy on teacher certification has been used as an important leverage to manipulate the quality of the teaching profession, and it is one of the most widely tested teacher attributes in educational research. The extant evidence indicates a relationship between certification in mathematics and students' high school mathematics achievement; however, there is little evidence of this association to student achievement in lower grades of mathematics (Rice, 2003). Rowan, Correnti, and Miller (2002) used three-level hierarchical linear modeling to examine the impact of teacher certification on elementary student achievement gains in mathematics and reading. The study found no apparent influence from teacher certification. In a different study focusing on high school level, among a range of teacher inputs, teacher certification was the most significant factor that contributed to student mathematics achievement at tenth grade (Goldhaber & Brewer, 1997b).

Another value-added study found having full certification (effect size = 0.09, p <0.01, 2.4% of the classroom-level variance) was the only teacher background variable (versus teaching experience and race) associated with reading achievement gains during first grade, and none was significantly associated with math achievement gains (Palardy & Rumberger, 2008). This study conducted a post-hoc analysis to examine whether fully certified teachers differ from those with less than full certification on key variables, such as instructional behavior and attitudes. The results showed that teachers in these two certification categories used surprisingly similar classroom practices. In addition, there was no significant difference in attitudes, such as efficacy and expectations.

Types of teacher certification also have been studied at several levels. Goldhaber and Brewer (2000) examined how student performance on twelfth-grade mathematics related to various teacher certification statuses: standard certification, probationary certification, emergency certification, private school certification, and no certification in subject area taught. They found teachers holding standard certification have a positive impact on student test scores compared with those holding no certification or private school certification. Interestingly, they also found little difference in student performance in mathematics between teachers who acquire alternative-route certification and those with standard certification. However, a study in Houston, Texas (Darling-Hammond, Holtzman, Gatlin, & Heilig, 2005) used a sample of 4,408 teachers in grades 4 and 5 from 1996–97 school year to the 2001–02 school year, and found that the teachers with standard certification and more education training do better in producing student achievement compared to uncertified teacher and those with nonstandard certification. Figure 4.4 summarizes the findings regarding the impact of teacher certification status on student achievement.

Figure 4.4. General Findings Regarding Impact of Teachers' Certification Status on Student Achievement

Type of Coursework	Impact on Student Achievement
Certification in mathematics for high school teaching	Positive impact
Certification in mathematics for elementary school teaching	No impact
Standard certification versus no certification, partial certification, or emergency certification	Positive impact
Standard certification versus alternate-route certification	Inconclusive (variable results)

Content Knowledge

Researchers have addressed the issue of teacher content knowledge through the measurement of coursework, questionnaire, and observation. The literature has been consistent in the findings about the positive association between teacher content knowledge and students' learning at all grade levels, particularly in mathematics.

Students whose teachers answered a high school-level mathematics test item correctly made larger mathematics gains between eighth and tenth grades, even after controlling for whether teachers held mathematics-related degrees (Rowan, Chiang, & Miller, 1997). Harris and Sass (2007) used panel data on all public school students and teachers in Florida for two time periods (1995–96 and 2003–04) to examine the relationship between teacher education and student achievement. They found teachers' pedagogical content knowledge positively associated with student test scores at the elementary and middle school levels but only in mathematics.

Hill, Rowan, and Ball (2005) examined first and third graders' achievement gains in mathematics. They found that teachers' mathematical knowledge significantly contributed to student mathematics learning, after controlling for other key student- and teacher-related characteristics. Insightfully, Hill et al. cautioned that effectiveness in teaching resides not simply in the knowledge a teacher has accrued, but how this knowledge is used in classrooms. For instance, teachers highly proficient in mathematics or writing will help others learn mathematics or writing only if they are able to use their own knowledge to enact learning activities that are appropriate to students. Figure 4.5 summarizes the findings regarding the impact of content and pedagogical knowledge on student achievement.

Figure 4.5. General Findings Regarding Impact of Teachers' Knowledge on Student Achievement

Type of Knowledge	Impact on Student Achievement
Content knowledge in mathematics	Positive impact
Pedagogical knowledge in mathematics	Positive impact

Note: Although extant studies point to the positive impact of teachers' mathematics knowledge on student achievement in math, it may be that this relationship in other content areas has not been demonstrated because of insufficient research to date.

Teaching Experience

Teacher experience is a crucial criterion for teacher compensation in most public school systems. Moreover, policy makers and researchers have shown increasing interest in investigating its impact on student achievement. Putting all evidence together, it seems that teachers' experience matters only for the first few years of teaching—in particular, the first three years. During these first few years, teachers appear to gain cumulatively in their contribution to student learning. After three years, however, the contribution of experience to student learning levels off.

A hierarchical linear model study by Munoz and Chang (2007) evaluated the effects of teacher characteristics in high school reading achievement gains using a multilevel growth model in a large urban school district. Thus, unlike most research on teacher characteristics from the past, Munoz and Chang used more than two data points to develop a growth model. The authors found that teaching experience is not predictive of student growth rates in high school reading. At the elementary school level, a value-added study by Heistad (1999) also found no significant correlation between teacher experience and student achievement—the effectiveness of second grade reading teachers was independent of their years of service.

Rockoff (2004) found that teaching experience significantly raises student test scores for both reading and math computation (but not math concepts) at the elementary level, particularly in reading subject areas. Ten years of teaching experience is expected to raise vocabulary and reading-comprehension test scores, respectively, by about 0.15 and 0.18 standard deviations. Put another way, on average, reading test scores differ by approximately 0.17 standard deviations between beginning teachers and teachers with ten or more years of experience. For mathematics subject areas, the effects of experience are smaller. The first two years of teaching experience appear to raise scores significantly in math computation. However, in this study, subsequent years of experience appear to have a negative impact on test scores (a counterintuitive finding).

Employing similar research methodology, Rivkin, Hanushek, and Kain (2005) noted that at the elementary level, teacher effectiveness increased during the first year or two but leveled off after the third year. Hanushek, Kain, O'Brien, and Rivkin (2005) linked student achievement in fourth- through eighth-grade mathematics with teacher characteristics, including teacher certification exam scores, educational attainment, teacher race, and experience. They found teacher experience associated positively with student achievement gains but only for the first few years.

Although the extant research generally supports the impact of teaching experience on student learning only for the first few years, this issue remains to be further explored. There are some studies that suggest a longer impact on student achievement. Additionally, studies outside of education have found that, in general, it can take ten years for professionals in complex jobs (e.g., medicine) to reach mastery (Cloud, 2008). Interestingly, a recent study revealed that type of experience, rather than total years of experience, is important for effectiveness (Huang & Moon, 2009). Specifically, teaching experience at grade level had a much larger effect on student achievement than overall years of experience. Figure 4.6 summarizes the findings regarding the impact of teaching experience on student achievement.

Figure 4.6. General Findings Regarding Teaching Experience on Student Achievement

Teaching Experience	Impact on Student Achievement
Years 1–3	Positive impact
Years >3	Inconclusive
Teaching experience in a given grade	Positive impact

Summary: A Priori Background Qualities and Student Achievement

Although the research has not generated a solid connection between the measurable teacher background characteristics and student learning, particularly in nonmathematics subjects, these attributes have been the driving criteria used for identifying effective teachers in educational policies as expressed in uniform teacher salary schedules. United States federal law emphasizes the need for states and districts to ensure that *all* students—particularly at-risk students, minority students, and students who are disadvantaged in various respects—have access to highly qualified teachers. For example, under *No Child Left Behind* (NCLB), every state was required to develop and implement a plan to ensure that all students will be taught by a "highly qualified teacher" (U.S. Department of Education, 2001).

Rockoff (2004) cautioned that policies that reward teachers based on conventional qualifications (e.g., certification and teaching experiences) may be less effective than policies based on less-measurable teacher characteristics, like classroom performance. This caution also was resonated by other empirical studies (e.g., Munoz & Chang, 2007; Rivkin, Hanushek, & Kain, 2005), finding that variance in student achievement is not attributable to easily measurable teacher characteristics, like degree and certification status. The research seems to be in agreement that NCLB provisions on highly qualified teachers are insufficient for ensuring that classrooms are led by highly effective teachers.

Palardy and Rumberger (2008) suggested that "ensuring that classrooms are led by highly effective teachers will require going beyond the screening of teachers based on background qualifications to implementing policies aimed at improving *teaching* effectiveness" (p. 129). This implies that more policy attention should be directed toward efforts to improve effectiveness once teachers are in service, rather than just focusing on teachers' prior-to-service characteristics.

Teacher Dispositions

Although teachers vary significantly in their ability to improve student achievement gains, little of this variation can be attributed to observable characteristics such as degree and teaching experience (Rivkin, Hanushek, & Kain, 2005). Rivkin et al. found that the difference in background qualities between new and experienced teachers accounted for only 10 percent of the teacher quality variance in mathematics and somewhere between 5 and 20 percent of the variance in reading. Thus, most of the qualities that make teachers effective are a result of other, less-researched differences among teachers. Goldhaber (2002) reached a similar conclusion. He pointed out that only approximately 3 percent of the contribution teachers make to student learning is associated with teacher experience, educational level, certification status, and other readily observable characteristics. The remaining 97 percent of teachers' effects on student achievement are associated with intangible, unobserved aspects of teacher quality such as dispositions, attitudes, and classroom practices (Figure 4.7).

Figure 4.7. Amount of Variability in Student Achievement Explained by Teacher Characteristics.

Variance in Student Achievement Explained by the Teacher

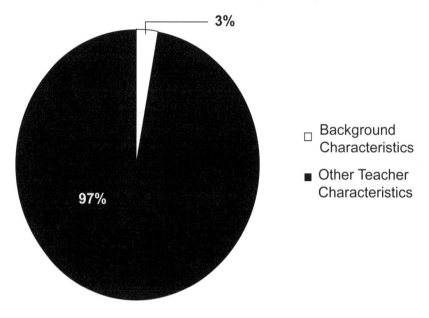

Adapted from Goldhaber, 2002.

Carter (2003) used multiple data-collection instruments, such as surveys, interviews, observations, and personal records, to develop a better understanding about the characteristics and dispositions of ninety-nine effective teachers. When these teachers were asked to list three characteristics of exceptional teachers, the most mentioned themes were as follows:

♦ Flexible, adaptable, will search for what works

♦ Excellent management skills, organized, discipline issues, etc.

♦ Caring, compassionate

♦ Loves working with children, loves children

♦ Believes all children can learn at high levels, high expectations

When these effective teachers were asked to report two strengths they possess. The most frequently mentioned strengths included having classroom management skills and organization; being hard-working and dedicated; possessing excellent communication skills; being enthusiastic and energetic; and being caring and kind (Carter, 2003).

Caring and Respectful Teachers

Caring about students and respecting them as individuals are prevalent in the literature descriptions of effective teachers. In particular, effective teachers are described as warm, friendly, and caring. Conversely, ineffective teachers often are said to create a tense classroom and are described as cold, abusive, and uncaring (Walls, Nardi, von Minden, & Hoffman, 2002). A study by Stronge, Ward, Tucker, and Hindman (2008) divided teachers into quartiles based on student achievement gains. Five highly effective teachers and six less-effective teachers participated in a cross-case analysis, including classroom observations, interviews, and other instructional analyses. The researchers found there was a difference in the overall personal qualities between the effective teachers and the ineffective teachers studied: the effective teachers demonstrated more respect and caring for students than did the less-effective teachers.

Effective teachers use care and respect to build relationships with their students that are conducive to academic learning. When students perceive that their teachers care about them, they respond by "optimizing their commitment to learning and putting forth greater efforts to reach their potential" (Lumpkin, 2007, p. 160).

Teacher Efficacy Beliefs

Effective teaching requires teachers who not only have efficacy beliefs about themselves but also the entire faculty. Research indicates that teachers' self-efficacy is an important variable in student learning. Goddard, Hoy, and Hoy (2004) used hierarchical linear model to eliminate the effects of student race, gender, socioeconomic status, and school size, so as to focus on the association between teacher collective efficacy and student achievement in elementary level mathematics and reading. The findings supported the role of collective efficacy in promoting school achievement. More studies in the same line of inquiry have consistently supported the association between teacher collective efficacy and teacher success (Hoy, Sweetland, & Smith, 2002; Goddard, LoGerfo, & Hoy, 2004). In addition, researchers found positive associations between student achievement and three types of teacher beliefs: academic emphasis, faculty trust in students and parents, and teachers' collective efficacy beliefs about the school system (Hoy, Tarter, & Hoy, 2006).

Motivation and Enthusiasm to Teach

Rowan, Chiang, and Miller (1997) examined to what extent the effects of teachers on student mathematics achievement can be explained by their motivation. In this study, teachers' motivation was measured by (1) teachers' general force of motivation, which is assessed by items developed to measure three closely related constructs—teachers' self-efficacy, outcome expectations, and locus of control—and (2) teachers' expectations for students to go to college. Rowan et al. found that students whose teachers had higher general force of motivation did not have higher levels of mathematical achievement than did students whose teachers had lower general force of motivation. However, teachers' student-specific expectancy motivation did have a statistically significant effect on students' achievement. Specifically in this study, students whose mathematics teachers expected them to go to college outperformed students whose teachers did not expect them to go to college by approximately 0.07 standard deviations. This means students whose teachers had higher outcome expectations for them had higher levels of mathematics achievement than did students whose teachers did not hold such expectations for them.

Teacher interest or motivation is a significant factor in classroom success. Teacher interest typically is expressed in a range of teacher behaviors that are perceived to be conducive to student learning, such as enthusiasm in content area taught, interest about students' personal and developmental needs, participation in content-related activities outside of class time, and displaying value and emotion for students (Long & Hoy, 2006).

Kunter, Tsiam, Klusmann, Brunner, Krauss, and Baumert (2008) made a distinction between teachers' enthusiasm for subject matter of mathematics from enthusiasm for teaching mathematics, and investigated how they relate to instructional behaviors. They found that teachers who were more enthusiastic about teaching showed higher-quality instructional behavior than those who were more enthusiastic about mathematics, from both the teacher and the student perspectives. Specifically, the more teachers were interested in teaching (1) the more monitoring they reported; (2) the more cognitive autonomy support they claimed to provide for students; (3) the more social support provided for students; (4) the more monitoring perceived by the students; (5) the more social support perceived by students; and (6) higher levels of cognitive challenge reported by the students.

Summary: Teacher Personal Dispositions and Student Achievement

A report, released by the National Bureau of Economic Research, rendered a synthesized study on the chractertiscs we discussed above: teacher professional background qualities and teacher dispositions (Rockoff, Jacob, Kane, & Staiger, 2008). The research team surveyed more than 400 teachers entering the teaching profession in New York City in the 2006–07 school year. They examined the characteristics that are not typically examined by districts, such as general cognitive ability, content knowledge, personality traits, and feelings of self-efficacy, and analyzed the link between these characteristics and student math test scores. The research team found that, individually, those characteristics generally did not predict teacher effectiveness, but when categorized into cognitive and noncognitive skills, both categories were shown to have a modest, statistically significant positive relationship to student outcomes. The characteristics examined that belonged to "cognitive skills" included being a Teach For America (TFA) corp member, attending a more selective college, SAT math score, SAT verbal score, Raven IQ test scores, and math knowledge for teaching. And the category of "noncognitive skills" included extraversion, conscientiousness, personal efficacy, and general efficacy, among others. The findings of this study cleared up a little of the mystery overcasting the issue about whether teacher input variables impact student achievement. The factor analysis methodology employed in this study to group discrete teacher characteristics into larger components indicated that certain teacher characteristics are not quite predictive when they stand alone, while in combination, they can add value in predicting whether a teacher would be more effective in a classroom. These results suggest that, while making the decisions on hiring or evaluating teachers, we cannot depend upon one single factor to tell us whether they will succeed in teaching; however, using a set of measures can make that judgment much more informative and accurate.

How Do Teachers' Skills and Practices Affect Student Achievement?[3]

Although there is general agreement that teachers have a significant impact on student learning and teachers vary in their ability to help students learn, there is a lack of consensus about which aspects of teachers' instructional practices matter most. The research findings presented in this section focus on what Rowan, Correnti, and Miller (2002) referred to as "process variable," which was defined as "properties of the interactive phase of instruction—that is, the phase of instruction during which students and teachers interact around academic content" (p. 1538).

The Influence of a Combination of Teacher Skills and Practices on Student Achievement

The studies using multivariate analysis of naturalistic data on teacher qualifications, like degrees, years of service, and certification status, have not satisfactorily explained the variance in student achievement. Palardy and Rumberger (2008) used longitudinal student achievement data to investigate the importance of three general aspects of teacher effects—teacher background qualifications, attitudes, and instructional practices—to reading and math achievement gains in first grade. The results indicated that compared

---

3 For a more detailed discussion of teacher skills and practices, see Stronge (2007).

with attitudes and instructional practices, background qualifications have weak associations with achievement gains.

Classroom Management

Classroom management includes actions taken by teachers to establish order, engage students, elicit student cooperation, with an ultimate purpose to establish and maintain an environment conducive to instruction and learning (Emmer & Stough, 2001). Two key features of effective classroom management are:

♦ Good management that is preventive rather than reactive; and

♦ Teachers who help create well-managed classrooms by identifying and teaching desirable behaviors to students.

Effective teachers were found to maintain their management system by "monitoring and providing prompt feedback, pacing class activities to keep them moving, and by consistently applying classroom procedures and consequence" (Emmer & Stough, 2001, p. 105).

Wang, Haertel, and Walberg (1994) analyzed a knowledge base comprising 11,000 statistical findings connecting a variety of variables and student achievement in order to answer the question: *What helps students learn?* Twenty-eight categories of factors, classified into six broad types of influences (i.e., student aptitude, classroom instruction and climate, context, program design, school organization, state and district characteristics) were scored based on their positive impact on learning. Of the twenty-eight categories, classroom management ranked first and was the most influential variable, just ahead of student metacognitive processes and cognitive processes. In the researchers' view, "effective classroom management increases student engagement, decreases disruptive behaviors, and makes good use of instructional time" (p. 76). Their definition of effective classroom management included effective questioning/recitation strategies, learner accountability, smooth transitions, and teacher "with-it-ness."

Taylor, Pearson, Clark, and Walpole (1999) observed 104 kindergarten through third-grade teachers and then categorized them as "most accomplished," "moderately accomplished," and "least accomplished" based on the degree to which they demonstrated elements of effective instruction. They found the "most accomplished" were experts at classroom management. In general, they had well-established classroom routines and procedures for handling behavior problems, smooth transitions between activities, and a rapid rate of instruction, thus, allowing for high instructional density. They managed, on average, to engage virtually all (96 percent) of their students in the work of the classroom.

Stronge, Ward, Tucker, and Hindman (2008) found that compared with bottom-quartile teachers, top-quartile teachers (as determined by their ability to effect student achievement gains) were more organized than ineffective teachers with efficient routines and procedures for daily tasks. And they communicated higher behavioral expectations to students. The top teachers' classrooms also were found to have fewer disruptive student behaviors (once every two hours) than did the classrooms of less-effective teachers (a disruption every twelve minutes).

Allington and Johnston (2000) observed and interviewed thirty fourth-grade literacy teachers in twenty-four schools of five states, who were identified as exemplary through a snowball nomination process. These teachers' classroom talk was found to have the following characteristics:

- The classroom talk could be described as respectful, supportive, and productive and was not only modeled by the teacher in interactions with students, but also deliberately taught and expected.

- The talk between teacher and student was personalized and personal. Exemplary teachers used authentic conversation to learn about students. And they encouraged students to engage each other's ideas. The authority was more distributed than centralized.

- "No" or "Yes" were rarely uttered by the teachers except in response to gross social transgression.

- The classroom talk made genuine inquiry possible—indeed, common—and inquiry processes a normal topic of conversation.

Figure 4.8 summarizes key findings regarding classroom management.

Figure 4.8. Selected Findings Regarding Classroom Effectiveness and Student Achievement

Classroom Management Qualities

- Preventive discipline
- Teach students desirable classroom behaviors
- Monitoring student behavior
- Well-established rules and procedures
- Consistent application of rules and procedures
- High student engagement
- Positive, respectful, and supportive classroom talk

Planning for Instruction

A solid planning process is integral to a teacher's efforts in identifying appropriate curriculum, instructional strategies, and resources to address the needs of all students. Furthermore, teachers' planning influences the content of instruction, the sequence and cognitive demands of subject topics, learning activities and students' opportunities to learn, and the pacing and allocation of instructional time. Despite the importance of teacher planning practices, the research that investigates instructional planning is scarce. However, there does exist research evidence indicating a difference in planning behaviors adopted by effective and less-effective teachers.

Researchers in Wake County Public Schools (WCPSs), North Carolina, used a multiple regression analysis on state tests to identify the effectiveness of schools and teachers. Haynie (2006) examined practices of the ten most effective and ten least-effective biology teachers in WCPSs, who were identified by regression and residual analyses of standardized state testing results. Most top teachers collaborated with one or more teachers while planning lessons; however, the bottom teachers reported they always planned lessons alone. The top teachers also were not restricted by pacing guides, and reached beyond prepared resources to plan their own activities, while most bottom teachers used resources already prepared. Top teachers also used student assessment data in the planning of instruction. Based on data drawn from frequent assessments, they made data-driven decisions about what goals and objectives to address.

Allington and Johnston (2000) also found that the instruction of effective teachers was multisourced. Exemplary teachers were inclined to stretch the reading and writing beyond the textbooks. Although effective teachers often dipped into prescribed textbooks, they hardly ever followed traditional plans for these materials. For instance, while planning for a lesson in social science, the effective teachers usually used historical fiction, biography, information on the Internet and magazine, and other nontraditional content sources.

Borko and Livingston (1989) investigated the pedagogical expertise in instructional planning by comparing novice teachers with experienced teachers. They found that novices showed more time-consuming, less-efficient planning. While implementing the planned lessons, their attempts to be responsive to students were likely to lead them away from scripted lesson plans. The novice teachers were less successful in translating their instructional plans into actions than were expert teachers. The expert teachers were better able to predict where in a course the students were likely to have problems and predict misconceptions the students would have and areas of learning these misconceptions were likely to affect. Figure 4.9 summarizes key aspects of effective teachers' instructional planning practices.

Figure 4.9. Selected Findings Regarding Instructional Planning and Student Achievement

Instructional Planning Qualities

- Collaboration in planning with other teachers
- Planning not limited to traditional resources (e.g., curriculum, textbooks)
- Data-driven planning
- Efficiency in translating plans into actions
- Ability to predict in planning troublesome areas for student learning

Implementing Instruction

An array of studies have found that the actual practice of teaching is a critical factor for student learning (Palardy & Rumberger, 2008; Rowan, Correnti, & Miller, 2002; Stronge, Ward, Tucker, & Hindman, 2008). Teachers with the same background qualifications and same schooling resources do different things in their classrooms and, consequently, enable their students to achieve at different levels. To discover what makes a teacher effective, we need to look closely into the black box of the classroom and see how teachers translate their content knowledge, pedagogical skills, and resources into opportunities for student learning.

Cohen, Raudenbush, and Ball (2003) proposed a model in which the key causal agents for student achievement reside in instruction. Said differently, instruction has immediate causal effects on student learning. A similar point was made by Palardy and Rumberger (2008), who noted that of the three aspects of teachers discussed in this chapter—background qualifications, personal dispositions such as attitudes, and instructional practices—instructional practices have the most proximal association with student learning. That is, "instructional practices are theorized to influence student learning directly, whereas teacher background qualifications and teacher attitudes are theorized to influence learning indirectly through their association with instructional practices" (p. 115).

Unfortunately, compared to the plentiful large-scale research on teachers' background characteristics, the empirical studies examining the connection between measured classroom practices and student achievement are scarce. Nonetheless, the studies that have been conducted have found substantial effects of teacher practices on student learning, and find that instructional effects are considerably larger than those of background characteristics.

Based on a synthesis of thousands of studies on student achievement, Hattie (2003) suggested that teachers account for 30 percent of student achievement variance. However, little of the teacher effects can be attributed to observable characteristics such as education or experience and most is a result of unobserved differences in instructional quality. Thus, teachers' practices inside the classrooms have not only statistical but also practical significance on student learning. Figure 4.10 summarizes the literature review conducted by Hattie (2003) on a range of school factors that relate to student achievement. The elements highlighted are descriptors of teacher classroom-level instructional practice and their corresponding effect size.

Figure 4.10. Impact of Teacher Practices on Student Achievement

Variables	Effect Size	Source of Influence
Providing formative evaluation	0.90	Teacher
Acceleration	0.88	School
Teacher clarity	0.75	Teacher
Feedback	0.73	Teacher
Teacher-student relationships	0.72	Teacher
Metacognitive strategies	0.69	Teacher
Students prior achievement	0.67	Student
Self-verbalization/self-questioning	0.64	Teacher
Note labeling students	0.61	Teacher
Problem-solving teaching	0.61	Teacher
Direct Instruction	0.59	Teacher
Mastery learning	0.58	Teacher
Concept mapping	0.57	Teacher
Socioeconomic status	0.57	Home
Class environment	0.56	Teacher
Challenge of goals	0.56	Teacher
Peer tutoring	0.55	Teacher
Parental involvement	0.51	Home
Expectations	0.43	Teacher
Matching style of learning	0.41	Teacher

Variables	Effect Size	Source of Influence
Cooperative learning	0.41	Teacher
Advance organizers	0.41	Teacher
Questioning	0.46	Teacher
Peer effect	0.38	Student
Time on Task	0.38	Teacher
Computer-assisted instruction	0.37	Teacher
Testing	0.34	Teacher
Homework	0.29	Teacher
Aims & policy of the school	0.24	School
Affective attributes of students	0.24	Student
Finances	0.23	School
Individualization	0.23	Teacher
Teaching test taking and coaching	0.22	Teacher
Physical attributes of students	0.21	Student
Personality	0.19	Student
Family structure	0.17	Home
Ability grouping	0.18	School
Reducing class size from 25 to 13	0.13	School
Teacher subject-matter knowledge	0.09	Teacher
Student control over learning	0.04	Teacher
Retention	−0.16	School
Television	−0.18	Home

Adapted from Hattie (2003, 2009).

Assessment for Learning

The practice of assessing student progress is essential for effective instruction and learning. It provides teachers with the information regarding the extent to which students have attained the intended learning outcomes, and it informs teachers' instructional decision making (what to teach and how to teach) as well. The goals of assessment are to provide teachers with day-to-day data on students' mental preparedness for certain learning targets and to facilitate teachers in making data-based decisions for instruction modification. The data can come from small-group discussion with the teacher and a few students, whole-class discussion, journal entries, portfolio entries, exit cards, skill inventories, pretests, homework assignments, student opinion, or interest surveys (Tomlinson, 1999).

Based on a large-scale research review, Hattie (2003) found that compared to their ineffective colleagues, effective teachers were adept at monitoring student problems and assessing their level of understanding and progress, and they provided much more relevant, useful feedback. The research also shows that effective teachers were more adept at developing and testing hypotheses about learning difficulties or instructional strategies. Wenglinsky (2002) found that teachers' use of frequent assessment and constructive feedback had a positive effect on student mathematics and science achievement at all grade levels. Another research team noted that effective teachers and ineffective teachers differed in their student assessment practices (Stronge, Ward, Tucker, & Hindman, 2008). For instance, the effective teachers were found to provide more differentiated assignments for students than those deemed ineffective.

Student progress monitoring is a practice that helps teachers use student performance data to continuously evaluate the effectiveness of their teaching and make more informed instructional decisions (Safer & Fleischman, 2005). To implement student progress monitoring, the teacher first preassesses a student's current competency level on skills covered by the curriculum, sets up ultimate achievement goals for the school year, and establishes the rate of progress the student must make to attain those goals. Then the teacher uses ongoing, frequent, brief, and easily administered measures to monitor the student's academic progress (Safer & Fleischman, 2005). Fuchs, Deno, and Mirkin (1984) used an experimental design to investigate the effects of frequent curriculum-based assessments. Thirty-nine special education teachers in the area of reading were randomly assigned to a repeated curriculum-based assessment group and a conventional assessment group, and each teacher selected three or four students for this project. Over the eighteen-week implementation, pedagogical decisions were surveyed; instructional structure was observed and measured; and students' knowledge about their learning was assessed through an interview. Analyses indicated that:

♦ Teachers in the experimental group who adopted systematic assessment procedures, effected greater student achievement than did those who used conventional monitoring methods.

♦ Teachers in the experimental group had more improvement in their instructional structure.

♦ Experimental group teachers' pedagogical decisions reflected greater realism and responsiveness to student progress.

♦ The students taught by experimental group teachers were more knowledgeable of their own learning and more conscious of learning goals and progress.

Student progress monitoring facilitates teachers tracking students' academic growth on a regular basis. It can continually provide teachers with the data and evidence about students' performance to evaluate the effectiveness of their instruction and make adjustments in their pedagogical behavior.

Teachers who monitor their students' progress exhibit greater concerns about student learning and higher academic emphasis in their instruction. They also are better at supervising the adequacy of student learning, identifying students in need of additional or different forms of instruction, and determining what instructional modifications are necessary. Progress monitoring also can help teachers set meaningful student achievement goals to tap into greater student potential of learning. Empirical research found that when progress monitoring is combined with goal-raising, student learning profiles, and appropriate instructional modifications, it could help teachers build stronger instructional programs that are more varied and more responsive to students' learning needs, and effect better academic performance for students (Fuchs & Fuchs, 2003). Stecker, Fuchs, and Fuchs (2005) noted that teachers effected significant growth in student learning with progress monitoring only when they modified instruction based on progress monitoring data; however, frequent progress monitoring alone did not boost student achievement. Figure 4.11 summarizes key findings related to monitoring student progress and potential.

Figure 4.11. Selected Findings Regarding Monitoring Student Progress and Student Achievement

Monitoring Student Progress

♦ Uses frequent assessment

♦ Provides constructive feedback

♦ Informs instructional decision making

♦ Uses data-based decisions for instruction modification

♦ Leads to differentiated assignments

♦ Assesses instructional effectiveness

So What Makes Good Teachers Good?
Putting the Evidence Together

Studies on teacher effectiveness have provided some insights into the qualities that connect teacher effectiveness and student achievement. The outcomes of these studies, while informative, have not led to a standard definition of teacher effectiveness. Neither have they generated a commonly agreed-upon list of effective teaching qualities. Generally, effective teachers plan carefully, use appropriate materials, communicate goals to students, maintain a brisk pace, assess student work regularly, reteach material differently if students have trouble, and so forth. They use class time well and have coherent strategies for instruction. They hold the expectations that their students can learn and they believe they have a large responsibility to help (Cohen, Raudenbush, & Ball, 2003). And this list is far from complete. In essence, teaching is highly complex work with a multitude of teacher-related, as well as other, variables affecting student success.

Caveat: Complexities of Classroom Instruction

Researchers of classroom-level education have been striving to pin down the relationship between attributes of teachers (either the easily measurable background characteristics or the intangible variables like attitudes, as well as instructional practices) and student achievement. This spectrum of research derives from the research paradigm of process-product research. Hill, Rowan, and Ball (2005) noted, "critiques of process-product studies ranged from methodological (e.g., an excessive reliance on correlational data) to conceptual. Chief among the conceptual critiques was the lack of attention given in these studies of subject matter and to how the subject being taught influenced the findings. What worked well to increase student achievement in mathematics, for instance, often did not work well to produce achievement gains in reading" (p. 374).

Although there is abundant research on teacher effectiveness, there remain many unanswered questions, including these:

♦ Are some teachers more effective in certain subject areas?

♦ Are some teachers more effective at certain grade levels?

♦ Are some teachers more effective with students from different backgrounds?

♦ Are some instructional strategies more effective with students of different learning abilities? (Rowan, Correnti, & Miller, 2002)

The answers for all these questions likely are "yes." Although teacher instructional practices within the walls of a classroom are believed to be more proximally associated with students learning, this association is moderated by certain aspects of the classroom, such as classroom demographic composition, student prior achievement, and peer effects. Schalock, Schalock, Cowart and Myton (1993) noted that simplistic conceptions of a teacher as an artist, as applied scientist, as decision maker, or as reflective practitioner fail to portray the complexity of teaching. Effective teaching is much more than implementing a number of pedagogical principles and content knowledge. It involves a dynamic interplay among content to be learned, pedagogical methods to be applied, characteristics of learners, and the context in which the learning is to occur. Schalock et al. found:

◆ "Large differences in effectiveness occur across teachers in their ability to impact student learning. This is true across subjects and across areas of learning within a subject." (p. 117)

◆ Many different types of learning take place within a particular subject, and many types of teaching are required to achieve desired outcomes. Teachers are not equally adept at fostering all types learning that need to occur within a particular subject.

◆ Teachers have differential success in fostering learning for groups of students within a classroom who differ in their level of prior academic achievement. For some teachers, the learning growth in their classroom may be concentrated in only a portion of students at a specific achievement level.

Rowan, Chiang, and Miller (1997) found the average levels of ability of students in a school conditions the effects sizes of teacher/school-level variables. This suggests there is an interactive relationship between student ability and teacher effectiveness qualities. Specifically, they found that classroom effects had only a moderate degree of consistency across different areas (i.e., reading and mathematics in this case), with correlations ranging from 0.30 to 0.47. This means that a given teacher varies in effectiveness when teaching different academic subjects, or even different content areas within the same subject. Rowan et al. also found classroom effects are influenced by different groups of students. Student background variables (socioeconomic status, gender, and minority status in this study) had different effects on annual gains in achievement across classrooms, with these random effects being larger in lower grades (especially in reading) than at upper grades.

Wayne and Youngs (2008) noticed an evolution of the conception about effective teachers as reflected in educational policies in the United States. For the most part of the twentieth century, as long as the candidates completed a state-approved teacher preparation program, they would be eligible for certification. In the 1980s, several states implemented performance assessments to see that teachers were equipped with a uniform set of teaching practices regardless of the content area or grade level they teach. Those practices were largely drawn from process-product research on teaching and were perceived to be evidence based. Over the past ten years, the standards used to look at teacher effectiveness have been more observant of the complexities of classroom teaching. In particular, these conceptions emphasize the context-specific nature of teaching and the need for teachers to integrate knowledge of subject matter, student, and context in making instructional decisions, engaging students in active learning, and reflecting on practice.

**Teaching is a Highly Complex
Concept and Practice**

Effective teaching is not simply a matter of implementing a small number of basic skills. Instead, effective teaching requires the ability to implement a large number of diagnostic, instructional, managerial, and therapeutic skills, tailoring behavior in specific contexts and situations to the specific needs of the moment. Effective teachers not only must be able to do a large number of things; they also must be able to recognize which of the many things they know how to do applies at the given moment and be able to follow through by performing the behavior effectively. (Brophy & Evertson, 1997, p. 139)

Conclusion

Despite the solid evidence on teacher qualities that so many researchers have assembled over the past several decades, there is no single set of teacher attributes that we can definitively point to and say: If a teacher has quality X, she will be an effective teacher. Nonetheless, we do know—without doubt—that if we are to improve our schools and positively influence student success, we have no choice but to look into classrooms, for is in the hard work of teachers in classrooms where our greatest hope for success lies.

5

How Does Teacher Effectiveness Impact School Reform?

Despite substantial increases in spending and many well-intentioned reform efforts, performance in a large number of school systems has barely improved in the past decades. Few of the most widely support-ed reform strategies (for instance, giving schools more autonomy, or reducing class size) have produced the results promised for them. Yet some schools systems consistently perform better and improve faster than others.

— Barber & Mourshed (2007, p.10)

Sometimes it feels as if we are continuously reforming public education, yet never changing it. What does it take to move beyond the promises and processes of reform to experience the real and lasting products of school improvement? How do we eliminate the Teflon-effect, in which all reform efforts simply slide off after a few months or a few years, and we find our-selves back at the beginning? What is needed for real and lasting reform to take deep root and then yield fruit?

This chapter focuses on the role that teachers play in school improve-ment. Specifically, two contemporary reform issues (class-size reduction and teacher pay) that have generated broad-based support are reviewed. Finally, extant research related to the overarching relationship between school reform and teacher quality is reviewed. With these issues in mind, guiding questions for Chapter 5 include the following:

♦ How does teacher quality relate to class-size reduction?

♦ How does teacher quality relate to teacher pay reform?

♦ Can school improvement succeed without teacher improvement?

How Does Teacher Effectiveness Relate to Class-Size Reduction?

Class-Size Reduction and Teacher Effectiveness

To illustrate the power of teacher quality on a reform such as class-size reduction, consider the relative impact of class reduction as compared to teacher performance improvement on student achievement. Various studies have found that reducing class size in primary grades from about twenty-three to twenty-four to fifteen can yield an effect size in the range of 0.15 to 0.26 (U.S. Department of Education, 1998). This translates, at best, to a 7 to 8 percentile point rise in achievement over the course of a year (Barber & Mourshed, 2007). A 7 to 8 percentile gain is a nice increase in student achievement, but it comes from one of the most expensive educational reform policies we can devise.

When juxtaposed with improving teacher quality, the effect of class-size reduction pales in comparison. For instance, in a large-scale study of students in Texas, Rivkin, Hanushek, and Kain (2005) found that the effects of a costly ten-student reduction in class size are smaller than the benefits of moving one standard deviation up the teacher-quality distribution. Figure 5.1 illustrates the relative impact of class-size reduction with the student achievement gains associated with improvement in teacher performance.

Teacher Effectiveness: Small Class Size Case Study

Using data from a four-year (kindergarten to grade 3) experiment in which teachers and students were randomly assigned to classes, known as the Tennessee Class Size Experiment, or Project STAR (Student–Teacher Achievement Ratio), Nye, Konstantopoulos, and Hedges (2004) conducted a detailed study that focused on estimating teacher effects on student achievement. The study involved students in seventy-nine elementary schools in forty-two school districts in Tennessee. Within each school, students were

Figure 5.1. Comparative Impact of Class-Size Reduction and Teacher Quality on Student Achievement

	Annual Student Achievement Gains
◆ Class size reduction: Reducing primary grade classes from larger sizes (22 to 26 students) to smaller sizes (13 to 17 students) (Nye, Hedges, & Konstantopoulos, 2001)	◆ + 2–6 percentile points
◆ Teacher quality improvement: Improvement from 25th percentile to 75th percentile in teacher effectiveness (Stronge, Ward, Tucker, & Grant, in review)	◆ +30 percentile points

randomly assigned to classrooms in one of the three treatment conditions: (1) small classes (with thirteen to seventeen students); (2) larger classes (with twenty-two to twenty-six students); or (3) larger classes with a full-time classroom aide. Teachers also were assigned randomly to these types of classes. Hierarchical linear modeling (HLM) was used to determine the achievement differences among entire classrooms of students. The classroom achievement differences were then used to explain the differences in teacher effectiveness.

Random assignment of students and teachers was considered very important for this study. If the classes within each school are initially equivalent (as a result of random assignment), then any systematic differences in mean achievement among classes can be attributed to one of two sources: (1) the treatment (small classes, larger classes, or larger classes with a full-time aide) or (2) differences in teacher effectiveness. Furthermore, if there is a systematic difference in achievement among classrooms that were assigned to the *same* treatment type within schools, then that difference can be attributed to the variance in teacher effectiveness. Statistical analyses confirmed that random assignment was successful in assuring there were no significant differences among students in terms of their socioeconomic status, ethnicity, and age across classrooms, across treatment types, and even across classrooms within the same treatment type. Furthermore, the analyses indicated that random assignment was successful in ensuring there were no statistical differences among teachers in terms of their race, experience, and education across treatment types.

The key findings from this study are instrumental in shedding light on the relative importance of class size versus teacher quality. Specifically, key findings that emerged from the study included:

◆ Variation in class size cannot explain variance across teachers in student achievement or achievement gains.

◆ The effect of one standard deviation change in teacher effectiveness is larger than that of reducing class size from twenty-five to fifteen (a finding consistent with the Rivkin, Hanushek, and Kain, 2005, study cited earlier).

Additional Findings for Teacher Effectiveness: Small Class Size

The one policy almost every school system has pursued in recent years is reducing class size. Class-size reduction, facilitated by lower student-to-teacher ratios, has probably been the most widely supported and most extensively funded policy aimed at improving schools.

— Barber & Mourshed (2007, p. 11)

Project STAR focused strictly on class-size reduction, and did not provide special training or professional development to teachers or aides (Finn, 2002). Munoz (2001) found no impact on student learning as measured by standardized mathematics and reading tests after a one-year class reduction in the third grade of the Jefferson County Public Schools in Louisville, Kentucky. The researcher observed, "A one-year intervention does not produce immediate results in student learning." He also concluded that more attention should have been paid to the training and experience of teachers, and to the professional and curriculum development that might have helped them make the most of smaller classes (Munoz, 2001).[1]

Figure 5.2 provides an overview of key findings from selected studies that summarize the relationship between teacher quality and class-size reduction initiatives.

The available evidence suggests that the main driver of the variation in student learning at school is the quality of the teacher (Barber & Mourshed, 2007). Furthermore, not only does teacher effectiveness have more impact on student achievement than class size, it also seems be more cost-effective than reducing class size, from the perspective of cost-benefit analysis on educational reform. Although the costs of class-size reduction have not been thoroughly and accurately estimated, they are likely to surpass the costs on improving teacher quality to achieve the same amount of student learning

---

1 As a side note, this study contributed to winning the American Evaluation Association 2001 Marcia Guttentag Award.

Figure 5.2. Selected Findings on Teacher Quality and Class-Size Reduction

Study	Key Findings
Hanushek, Kain, & Rivkin, 1998	◆ "The evidence on class size is somewhat mixed: there is a statistically negative relationship between class size and math and reading achievement in 4th and 5th grade but not in 6th grade" (p. 24). ◆ "Class size explains less than 0.1 percent of the total variation in achievement gains and less than 0.5 percent of the between school and year variance of test score gains in all specifications. Thus the contribution of class size to the variation in achievement gains is less than one-twentieth of the contribution of teacher quality differences despite the substantial class size differences within schools" (p. 30). ◆ Smaller class sizes have more positive effect for low-income students in earlier grades. ◆ The effects of teaching experience and class size explain only a small amount of the total observed variation in teacher quality.
Rivkin, Hanushek, & Kain, 2005	◆ Class size has small, but significant effects on both mathematics and reading achievement gains in 4th and 5th grade, but the impact declines markedly as students progress through schools and tends to be less significant in reading than in mathematics. The effects of class size are not substantially larger for disadvantaged students. ◆ The effects of a costly ten-student reduction in class size are smaller than the benefits of moving one standard deviation up the teacher quality distribution.
Barber & Mourshed, 2007	◆ Except at the very early grades, class-size reduction does not appear to have much impact on student outcomes. ◆ Of 112 studies that looked at the impact of the reduction in class size on student outcomes, only 9 found any positive relationship; 103 found either no significant relationship, or a significant negative relationship. ◆ Every single one of the studies showed that within the range of class sizes typical in Organization for Economic Co-operation and Development (OECD) countries, "variations in teacher quality completely dominate any effect of reduced class size" (p. 11).

outcome. There are several reasons to support the different productivity of these two educational inputs (Rivkin, Hanushek, & Kain, 2005). First, class-size reduction leads to more costly expenditures, for instance, increased building requirements. Second, class-size reduction requires expansion of the teacher work force to fill in the smaller classes, which, in turn, increases salary demands. Additionally, because the supply of teachers is not perfectly elastic, the increased demand on the teacher workforce most probably will lead to decreased teacher quality, at least in the short run.

Despite the evidence cited above, I am not advocating foregoing class-size reduction and similar initiatives; rather, I am merely pointing out that teacher quality can—and will—have an overwhelming impact on the success or failure of school reforms. It is worth noting that the effects of small class size persist into later grades and are particularly beneficial to poor and minority students (Odden, Borman, & Fermanich, 2004). Indeed, smaller classes can pay dividends, but without the most capable and committed teachers in those smaller classes, we will never see their true potential unlocked.

Can School Improvement Succeed Without Teacher Improvement?

It appears that few, if any, school-level reforms or improvement plans can bring forth the intended changes in student achievement unless they can make a difference in teacher effectiveness. To illustrate, some expensive innovations, like the $1.6 billion Comprehensive School Reform, were found to be not cost-effective in engendering improved student academic performance (Gross, Booker, & Goldhaber, 2009). Furthermore, studies have indicated school-level reform on instruction, without directly tackling the issue of teacher classroom effectiveness, generally have no detectable association with higher student achievement (Le, Lockwood, Stecher, Hamilton, & Martinez, 2009).

Hiring and Retaining the Best Teachers

Educators increasingly emphasize the significance of linking teacher effectiveness to various aspects of district/school personnel administration, including:

♦ Recruiting and inducting potentially effective teachers,

♦ Designing and implementing professional development,

♦ Conducting valid and credible evaluations, and

♦ Dismissing ineffective teachers and retaining effective ones (Hanushek, 2008; National Academy of Education, 2008; Odden, 2004).

This type of alignment is receiving increasing attention as an important means for providing quality education to all students and improving school performance.

Removing Low-Performing Teachers

Clearly, hiring, supporting, and retaining the highest quality teachers possible is the key to school improvement. However, we also need to consider the impact of low-performing teachers. Unfortunately, ineffective teachers have considerable negative impact on student achievement. Hanushek (2008) estimated that that if the average learning growth made by students each academic year is equivalent to one grade, then the teachers from the bottom 5 percent of the distribution can at best make two-thirds of a grade growth for their students. Because of the residual and cumulative effects of teacher quality, the learning of students who are assigned to the bottom 5-percent teachers for a few years in a row would be damaged permanently. Furthermore, Hanushek (2008) posited that if the bottom 6 to 10 percent of teachers in terms of effectiveness could be removed from classrooms, student achievement would increase by approximately one-half standard deviation. An increase of 0.5 standard deviation would move U.S. students much closer to the top compared with other developed countries—approximately where Canadian students fall but slightly behind such countries as Finland and South Korea. Figure 5.3, on page 80, depicts graphically the relationship between removing ineffective teachers and the concomitant rise in student achievement. Relatedly, Gordon, Kane, and Staiger (2006) also estimated that if the Los Angeles school district were to drop the bottom quartile of teachers in terms of their value-added impact on student test scores in the first two years of teaching, the district could raise overall student achievement by 14 percentile points over twelve years.

Spillover Effect of Effective Teachers

Hiring and maintaining highly effective teachers not only have a positive impact on the learning of the students they teach, but also they have "spillover" effects on the achievement of the students taught by their colleagues. Jackson and Bruegmann (2009) found that for the average teacher in a grade with three other peers, replacing one peer with a more effective one (who had one standard deviation higher value-added effects estimate) will increase the teacher's own students' achievement scores by 0.86 percent of a standard deviation. Additionally, this type of spillover effect is cumulative over time. Also, less experienced teachers are particularly responsive to changes in peer quality. Bruegmann also posited the plausible explanations for this spillover effect could be peer learning, collective motivation, joint production, and shared resources.

**Figure 5.3. Impact of Removing Ineffective
Teachers on Student Achievement**

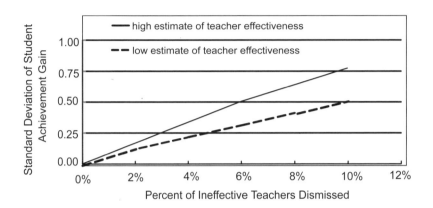

Adapted from Hanushek (2008).

How Does Teacher Effectiveness
Relate to Teacher Pay Reform?

At the heart of educational reform in the United States and, in fact, in virtually all nations in which systemic school improvement efforts have been undertaken in recent decades, are the interrelated goals of improving student achievement and ensuring high-quality teachers in every classroom. Given these twin goals of improving teacher quality and student performance, the rationale for restructuring the teacher compensation system in a nation, a state, or a single school system has been pushed to the forefront of reform. Many of these reforms aimed at connecting teacher quality and teacher pay address one, if not all, of three critically important teacher quality factors

♦ *Attracting* quality teacher candidates to the profession,

♦ *Developing* teachers across the career span, and

♦ *Retaining* quality teachers in the classroom (Stronge, Gareis, & Little, 2006).

Studies Connecting Teacher Pay and Teacher Effectiveness

In a longitudinal, value-added study in which the authors evaluated the effects of selected teacher characteristics, the researchers found that teacher education and teacher experience—two factors that traditionally have been used as the primary determinants for uniform teacher salary schedules—had very little explanatory value for teacher effectiveness (Munoz & Chang,

2007). Rather than an isolated finding, the Munoz and Chang study sets the tone for virtually every value-added study that addresses the connection between teacher pay and teacher quality.

The Munoz and Chang study also cautions that performance pay is controversial in that it bases teachers' pay on their productivity, not just on salaries set in advance. Some problems in performance-based compensation include the possibilities of teachers teaching to the tests that measure student performance, creating a competitive atmosphere that undermines the collegiality among teachers, and increasing teacher turnover in schools with struggling students (Guin, 2004). Yet, this private sector-driven school of thought claims that new compensation methods are necessary to improve the quality of teaching (Figlio, 2002).

Similar to the above-noted study, Rivkin, Hanushek, and Kain (2005) found in their Texas study of the connection between teacher effectiveness and student achievement that a substantial share of the overall achievement gain variation occurs between teachers. Thus, teachers have powerful effects on reading and mathematics achievement. Given these findings, they, too, suggested that linking teacher pay and teacher performance could be an effective way to improve teacher quality.

Again, in another value-added study investigating the effects of teachers on student achievement, an economist (Rockoff, 2004) estimated that a one-standard-deviation increase in teacher effects raises student test scores by approximately 0.1 standard deviations in reading and math on nationally standardized distributions of achievement. Discussing implications for teacher quality and teacher pay, he noted that:

♦ Raising teacher quality may be a key instrument in improving student outcomes.

♦ Policies that reward teachers based on credentials may be less effective than policies that reward teachers based on performance.

In an Australian study of teacher effects on study achievement, economist Andrew Leigh (n.d.) analyzed data from 10,000 Australian primary school teachers and more than 90,000 pupils to estimate teacher effectiveness as measured by gains made by the students taught by the teachers. He found that most of the differences among teachers were a result of factors not captured by the current salary schedules in Australia, which are largely based on experience and qualification. Consequently, he recommended that alternative salary structures should be considered.

In another value-added economics analysis—this time in Chicago—Aaronson, Barrow, and Sander (2007) agreed that the vast majority of the variation in teacher effects is unexplained by easily observable teacher characteristics, including those used in traditional human capital measures for determining compensation. Figure 5.4 offers an overview of the evidence linking teacher pay and teacher quality.

Figure 5.4. Teacher Pay and Teacher Effectiveness: Evidence from Value-Added Studies

Study	Study Sample: Teachers and Students	Key Findings
Munoz & Chang, 2007	58 grade 9 teachers and 1,487 students with 3 data points	Traditional compensation system systems that pay teachers based on education and years of experience will not necessarily result in an increase in student learning.
Rivkin, Hanushek, & Kain, 2005	More than 500,000 students in more than 3,000 schools of Texas	Much of teacher quality variation exists within rather than between schools. This suggests that uniform salary schedules do not capture well issues of teacher quality.
Leigh, n.d.	10,000 Australian primary-grade teachers and their students	The combination of qualifications, gender, age, experience, and other identifiable ratings account for less than 1/100th of the variance in teacher effectiveness.
Aaronson, Barrow, & Sander, 2007	Teachers and students in 88 Chicago high schools (9th grade)	Tenure, advanced degrees, and teaching certification explain roughly 1 percent of the total variation in estimated teacher quality.

In summary, both educators and economists who have researched the policy implications of teacher pay and teacher quality noted that *they should be linked.* In the following quote, Goldhaber (2002) went to the heart of the argument for carefully considering the evidence on teacher quality when deciding how to pay teachers:

> Teachers can have a profound effect on students, and school systems make a significant long-term investment when they hire teachers. Unlike other education investments, such as class size, which may be easily altered from year to year, the tenure system implies that the employment of an individual teacher is near permanent. For these reasons, the selection of teachers is of paramount importance. I would argue that this function of school systems receives too little attention at the local level....Second,

the lack of clear evidence on the effectiveness of teacher certification suggests that policy makers should continue experiments....Finally, the compensation structure used by virtually all school districts is not well aligned to promote the acquisition of skills found to influence student outcomes. For instance, data from the National Center for Education Statistics show that salary schedules provide pay premiums of about 11 percent for master's degrees and 17 percent for a doctorate. Generally, these premiums are received regardless of whether degrees are specific to the subjects in which teachers teach, despite the evidence that out-of-field degrees contribute little toward student achievement. (pp. 6–7)

Teacher quality matters; let's invest in what matters most.

Conclusion

It is interesting to note that a major effect of principals in changing school effectiveness is achieved by changing staff members; again, pointing to the power and importance of teachers on student achievement (Bembry, Jordan, Gomez, Anderson, & Mendro, 1998). Additionally, Bembry et al. found that teacher effectiveness remains relatively stable over time and largely immutable to typical approaches to change. This strongly suggests that—in addition to structural changes—any school reform effort must pay careful attention to the quality of teachers if school improvement is to be deep and lasting.

6

Why Teachers Do Matter Most

Even the most experienced teachers believe teaching is inherently difficult and that teachers never stop learning to teach. Teaching is hard work.

— Fullan & Hargreaves (1996, pp. 44–48, cited in Jackson & Davis, 2000, p. 141)

So what does the connection between teacher quality and student achievement really mean? First, the importance of teacher quality cannot be overstated (Goldhaber, 2002). Of all the factors within our control in the educational enterprise, teacher quality matters most. There is no other school-related factor that will touch the lives of students so profoundly. And if this is true, then, second, it is incumbent on us to ascertain what are those teacher qualities that make such a difference in students' academic lives. Finally, we must know what is good teaching, make the best possible choices in selecting good teachers, develop our teaching corps based on the qualities of teacher effectiveness, and then do all within our ability to retain the best teachers. This concluding chapter addresses practical implications of matters of teacher quality via the following guiding questions:

♦ Can schools improve without teacher quality?

♦ What are implications for having effective teachers in a school?

♦ Why must we value effective teachers?

Can Schools Improve Without Teacher Improvement?

Let's turn our attention to the question of can school improvement efforts yield fruit without a concomitant commitment to teacher improvement? Another way to frame this question is: *Can school turnaround happen without a focus on teacher quality?*

Impact of Teacher Quality on School Improvement

Teacher effects are large enough to dwarf effects associated with other educational variables or interventions. Given the evidence regarding the central role that teachers play in school success, it seems safe to say that reform cannot happen without teacher improvement. In fact, effective teachers can make poor reform efforts look good, while ineffective teachers can make promising reform efforts look bad (Mendro, Jordan, Gomez, Anderson, & Bembry, 1998a,b).

In value-added studies with teachers in Dallas, Texas, Mendro Jordan, Gomez, Anderson, and Bembry (1998a,b) found that the effects of teachers on student achievement were pervasive. Indeed, the effects were of sufficient magnitude that they overwhelm the effects of typical programs and treatments.

♦ "...[A]nd that the effects teachers have are on an order of magnitude which dwarfs the effects associated with curriculum, staff development, restructuring, and other types of educational interventions" (Mendro et al., 1998a, p. 1).

♦ Implication for educational evaluation and research: Teachers have a large effect on their students' achievement, which even overshadows the effect of a typical educational intervention or experiment. Therefore, when we evaluate an educational intervention or program, we must take the effectiveness level of the teachers into account, particularly when this evaluation occurs in an environment of intact classrooms and schools where experimental control on teacher effectiveness is not possible (Mendro, et al., 1998a).

International Comparative Studies and the Impact of Teacher Quality

Consider the following depressing results from school reform in the United States spanning the most recent three decades:

> The federal government, state governments, school boards, principals, teachers, teacher unions, listed companies, nonprofit organizations, and others launched tens of thousands of initiatives aimed at improving the quality of education in the nation's schools. Actual student outcomes, however, as measured by the Department of Education's own national assessment program, stayed almost the same. Though there was some improvement in mathematics, the reading scores of 9-year-olds, 13-year-olds and 17-year-olds remained the same in 2005 as they had been in 1980. (Barber & Mourshed, 2007, p.10)

Clearly, *reform effort* does not equal *reform results*. The United States was not the only country which had trouble improving its schools. Almost all countries in the Organization for Economic Co-operation and Development (OECD) substantially increased their spending on education over the past twenty-five years, as well as implemented large-scale reform initiatives to improve their schools. And the results of these concerted expenditures of money and effort? Very few of the school systems achieved significant improvements in student performance. In fact, results of national and international assessments are showing that many school systems' performance had either flatlined or deteriorated (Barber & Mourshed, 2007). The fact that many of these reform efforts, in the United States and in other developed countries, appear well conceived and far reaching in their objectives makes their failure all the more perplexing. Even in countries like England that reformed "the funding of schools, the governance of schools, curriculum standards, assessment and testing, the inspection of quality, the role of local government, the role of national government, the range and nature of national agencies, the relationships of schools to communities, school admissions...," results were paltry, at best (Barber & Mourshed, 2007, p. 10).

The available evidence suggests that the main driver of the variation in student learning at school is teacher quality. Without capable, committed, and caring teachers, we simply cannot achieve our lofty aims. Consistent with this premise, the OECD international comparative study noted above found that three things matter most for school reform and improvement (Figure 6.1):

Figure 6.1. Factors That Matter in School Improvement

International Study Factors That Yield Success in School Reform

1. Getting the right people to become teachers.

2. Developing them into effective instructors.

3. Ensuring that the system is able to deliver the best possible instruction for every child.

Source: Barber & Mourshed, 2007, p. 13

All three of these findings point to the power and impact of quality teachers. The OECD study revealed that top-performing school systems recruited their teachers from the top third of each cohort graduate from their schools: the top 5 percent in South Korea, the top 10 percent in Finland, and the top 30 percent in Singapore and Hong Kong (p. 14). Simply put, without effective teachers, other reforms don't work—at least not the way they were envisioned.

No improvement in teacher quality = no improvement in schools.

> High-quality instruction throughout primary school could substantially offset the disadvantages associated with low socioeconomic background.
> Rivkin, Hanushek, & Kain (2005)

What Are Implications for Having Effective Teachers in a School?

A Case Study

A comprehensive study with ninety-nine teachers from Hamilton County (Chattanooga),Tennessee, was conducted to build a better understanding about the traits and characteristics of teachers who were conceived as highly effective. The traits examined include teacher background data, educational philosophies, collegial experiences and coursework, and professional development experiences. Teachers who participated in the study had either high Tennessee Value-Added Assessment System (TVAAS) scores or were nominated by their principals as highly effective teachers. Data sources included surveys, inventories, questionnaires, interviews, observations, and personal records which contained information about college coursework, certifications, and degrees (Carter, 2003).

How Effective Teachers Become Effective

Before turning our attention to the role of effective teachers in schools, let's briefly discuss how they become effective. In particular, what experiences do highly effective teachers value in their own development?

The study revealed a number of fascinating details in the backgrounds of these effective teachers that related either directly or indirectly to their growth and development as teachers. When asked questions about their own development, a number of interesting themes emerged (Figure 6.2).

Figure 6.2. Emergent Themes Noted in the Development of Effective Teachers

Emergent Themes in Effective Teachers' Development	Percentages
When did you first become aware that you wanted to become a teacher?	◆ 23.9% decided in college ◆ 22.9% elementary school (6–12 years old) ◆ 18.8% high school (16–18 years old) ◆ 16.6% very young (less than 6 years old)
Are there other members of your family that are or have been teachers?	◆ 99% (Amazing!)
What are the most difficult obstacles that highly effective teachers must overcome?	◆ 38%: lack of time ◆ 32%: parents who do not support education ◆ 28%: problems kids bring to school ◆ 27%: self-induced personal pressure ◆ 22%: bureaucracy

The teachers in the study were asked to rate their professional development experiences in terms of how valuable they were in helping the teachers develop and improve their teaching skills. Figure 6.3 summarizes how much (or little) the teachers valued typical professional growth opportunities afforded to all teachers.

Figure 6.3. Effective Teachers' Perspectives on the Value of Selected Professional Experiences

Professional Experience	Rank	Mean	Responses
Help from peers	1	3.62	99
Personal professional development	2	3.34	95
Help from mentor	3	3.31	65
Student teaching	4	3.17	96
College courses	5	3.00	99
Help from consultants	6	2.83	94
System professional development	7	2.79	98

Note: Range was from 1 (poor) to 4 (excellent).

Next, the teachers rated the following professional development events in their educational careers with a five-point rating scale (from 1 [least valuable] to 5 [most valuable]): conference, workshops, mentors, college courses, in-service. Figure 6.4 summarizes the ratings.

Figure 6.4. Effective Teachers' Perspectives on the Value of Selected Professional Development Opportunities

Professional Development Event	Rank	Mean	Majority Responses
Conference	1	4.15	47.1% most valuable
Mentors	2	3.91	37.7% most valuable
Workshops	3	3.86	43.5% most valuable
College courses	4	3.18	34.6% somewhat valuable
In-service	5	3.13	38.5% somewhat valuable

As can be seen from the figures above, this group of effective teachers tended to rate more highly personalized learning experiences, such as working individually with peers and mentors or attending conferences selected by themselves, than those that were standardized for all teachers (e.g., college coursework, district staff development).

How Effective Teachers Influence Their Schools

So once they become effective, what roles do these teachers tend to fill in their schools? In addition to their own teaching responsibilities, the answer lies in a range of teacher leadership roles (Carter, 2003; Figure 6.5).

Figure 6.5. School Leadership Roles
Assumed by Effective Teachers

Leadership Role	Percentage of Participating Teachers
Teacher Mentor	74%
Committee Chairperson	61%
Grade Chairperson	53%
Team Leaders	37%
Other Leadership Capacities For example: ♦ Serving on school improvement teams ♦ Representing various school reform initiatives ♦ Serving on the local education association	47%

When asked what steps would they initiate to improve the effectiveness of teachers in their schools, these effective teachers responded:

- ♦ 39%: more social/collaborative time
- ♦ 22%: time for teachers to get together
- ♦ 21%: make sure teachers are valued/appreciated/empowered
- ♦ 18%: have teachers observe other teachers/schools
- ♦ 17%: improve attitude towards kids
- ♦ 17%: provide more class time/prep time

When asked how a principal can help a teacher to become more effective, they responded:

- ♦ 60%: be supportive/be there for the teacher/support staff with what they need

- 40%: help struggling teachers/give advice/identify strengths and weaknesses

- 28%: provide staff development opportunities/opportunities to learn

- 32%: constructive criticism and feedback

- 28%: visit classrooms

- 26%: be very aware of what is going on in the building, be visible

- 24%: allow teacher to model off of others

And, finally, when asked to consider the ultimate purpose of schools, the teachers gave straight-forward responses (Figure 6.6).

Figure 6.6. Effective Teachers' Perspectives Regarding the Purposes of Schools

What Are Important Student Outcomes or Goals of Schools?	Percentage of Participating Teachers
Become successful citizens (Make better citizens)	64%
Feel successful in some area (Cope and succeed when they graduate)	63%
Learn to learn (Life-long learner)	41%
Acquire adequate knowledge to pursue college or a vocation	36%
Become well-rounded individuals for the world ahead	30%

In summary, these teachers weren't just effective in their own classrooms where many were getting high student achievement gain scores; rather, they willingly and extensively shared their abilities with colleagues throughout their schools (Carter, 2003). They also seemed to know that teaching—that is, good teaching—is inherently challenging work. Furthermore, these effective teachers were central to the entire fabric of school success. In their absence, I can't help but ponder what would be the status of school improvement as a whole?

Why Must We Value Effective Teachers

The teacher is a person, not a product, and is more than the sum of the parts (Stronge, 2007). No single set of qualities can translate into a warm, caring, human being who is effective in teaching in all settings and in every way. Indeed, good teachers never stop growing and reinventing themselves.

When we think of the value of quality teachers, perhaps there is no better paradigm to consider than the potential for good they hold for the students who come under their teaching and guidance. Elliot Eisner (2004) provided just such a framework for understanding the good that teachers can do by describing what schools (i.e., teachers) should teach in preparing students for today and tomorrow. His recommendations included:

♦ Teaching judgment

- The problems that matter most cannot be resolved by formula, algorithm, or rule.

- Good judgment requires good reasons. The disposition and critical acumen that make good judgment possible are among the most important abilities that schools can cultivate in students.

♦ Teaching critical thinking

- Critical thinking invokes the ability to critique ideas and to enjoy exploring what one can do with them.

♦ Teaching meaningful literacy

- This is the ability to read and write.

- Literacy includes the ability to encode or decode meaning in any of the symbolic forms used in the culture.

Finally, Eisner advocated teaching for the future by stating that *preparation* for tomorrow is best served by meaningful education today. Judgment, critical thinking, literacy, vision for the future—aren't these among the attributes that help explain why we must value extraordinary teachers so highly?

Conclusion

What seems abundantly clear is that the quality of students' opportunity to succeed in school is closely tied to the quality of the teachers to whom they are assigned. Fortunately or unfortunately—depending on the effectiveness of the teacher to whom a student is assigned—learning opportunity and learning outcomes, to a substantial degree, appear to be the luck of the draw. If we are to improve our schools and, more importantly, improve the opportunities for success of our students, we must remove the factor of chance in teacher assignment. Rather, it is imperative that we place quality teachers in classrooms with all students everyday for thirteen years, kindergarten to high school graduation. This is why effective teachers = student achievement.

Part II

Resources
You Can Use

Value-Added Methods

How Value-Added Methods Work

William Sanders pioneered the value-added methodology used in education with his work on the Education Value-Added Assessment System (EVAAS; formally Tennessee Value-Added Assessment System [TVAAS]) using statistical mixed-model methodology to enable a multivariate, longitudinal analysis of student scale scores (see Sanders & Horn, 1994, 1997, 1998; Sanders, Saxton, & Horn, 1997). EVAAS is used widely in numerous U.S. states to examine the effectiveness of schools systems, schools, and teachers in helping students achieve academic gains. As an example of Value-Added Methods (VAM), EVAAS methodology features the following:

♦ Uses a mixed-model methodology that is intended to circumvent many of the problems associated with the use of student achievement data to assess school systems, schools, and teachers "…by relying on the scale scores that indicates gains students make from year to year, regardless of the point at which the student enters the classroom" (Sanders & Horn, 1994, p. 309).

♦ Uses long-term (at least three years) student norm-referenced scale scores, and is presented by the authors as a reliable method to provide an unbiased estimate of the effects of school systems, schools, and teachers on students' academic growth.

♦ Is intended to "eliminate (or at least trivialize) many of the cited impediments to incorporating student achievement data in an educational outcomes-based assessment system," such as missing student records, various modes of teaching, teachers changing assignment over years, transient students, regression to the mean (Sanders & Horn, 1994, p. 299).

The empirical research using value-added methodology has been particularly powerful in estimating the magnitude of teachers' effects on student learning, as well as in identifying which teachers are effective and which teachers are ineffective in raising student achievement when the curriculum is uniform across classrooms. This line of research also has provided a closer examination on what characteristics account for the variance of effectiveness among teachers.

Virtues of Estimating Teacher Effects by Using Value-Added Model

Value-added analyses on longitudinal student achievement data are viewed by many as a trustworthy and accurate way to measure the professional performance of an individual school and teacher (Walberg & Paik, 1997). In our accountability-driven educational system, value-added models can provide important technical levers for monitoring the productivity and cost-effectiveness of programs, interventions, and schools personnel.

William Sanders (2000) stated that "an accountability system that is based upon the rate of academic progress of populations of students is one that will hold people accountable for things over which they have control, rather than for things over which they do not" (p. 331). Although value-added estimates should not be the sole criterion to make high-stakes evaluation decisions, VAM still is a fair, direct, and objective measure to hold teachers and schools accountable, according to Sanders (2000). Within this methodology, students are tracked as individuals when they progress through school. Each student's trajectory of academic achievement is assessed and documented. Additionally, value added models can determine how much student learning growth can be attributed to districts, schools, teachers, and learners, themselves.

The tenets of value-added modeling on student achievement continue to gain support in the United States. The thirty-ninth annual Phi Delta Kappa/ Gallup Poll asked Americans the following question:

One way to measure a school's performance is to base it on the percentage of students passing the test mandated by the state at the end of the school year. Another way is to measure the improvement students in the school made during the year. In your opinion, which is the best way to measure the school's performance—the percentage passing the test or the improvement shown by the students? (Rose & Gallup, 2007, p. 35)

The vast majority (82%) of respondents reported that school effectiveness should be evaluated by the achievement growth made by students across time (Rose & Gallup, 2007).

The data and analyses embodied in value-added models can provide valuable information for school decision-making compared with traditional reporting of raw student achievement scores. For instance, district and school administrators can use value added results to identify areas of strength and weakness, conduct curricular planning or reform, implement program evaluation, and develop strategies to meet the needs of students while taking their background characteristics and academic attributes into account (Sanders, Saxton, & Horn, 1997). Additionally, teachers can use value-added reports to assess their own effectiveness as manifested by the academic progress of their students, and focus on the needs of each individual student to ensure that they receive the type of instruction they deserve (Callender, 2004).

Inexactness of Estimating Teacher Effects

Despite the promise of Value-Added Methods, we still are in the infancy of its use in education. Thus, we need to exercise appropriate and due caution in VAM use. One of the reasons for caution is the inexactness of determining the impact of teachers on student achievement.

In a study exploring the use of large-scale databases to measure teacher effects on student achievement, Rowan, Correnti, and Miller (2002) calculated a strong influence of the teacher (i.e., the classroom) on student learning:

> After controlling for student background variables, the classroom to which students were assigned in a given year accounted for roughly 60–61% of the reliable variance in students' rates of academic growth in reading achievement and 50–72% of the reliable variance in students' rates of academic growth in mathematics achievement. This yields...effect sizes ranging from 0.77–0.78 for reading growth, and 0.72–0.85 for mathematics growth. (p. 1532)

However, in arriving at these findings, they offered two important caveats related to the subject matter under consideration as well as the characteristics of the students, themselves. The findings of the VAM they used indicated that classroom effects had only a moderate degree of consistency across difference subject areas (reading and mathematics in their study), with correlations ranging from 0.30 to 0.47. Thus, "a given teacher varies in effectiveness when teaching different academic subjects" (or even different content areas within the same subject) (p. 1533). The classroom effects also were influenced by different groups of pupils, with background variables (i.e., socioeconomic status, gender, and minority status) having different effects on annual gains in achievement across classrooms, with these random effects being larger in lower grades (especially in reading) than at upper grades.

Issues Concerning Value-Added Model Data

When it comes to using value-added modeling for high-stakes purposes, we need to be cautious in interpreting and applying the information. Value-added systems may be a good approach at the school level, but at the teacher level, using value-added results to make personnel decisions would be more ambiguous (Viadero, 2008a).

One reason that some policy makers and researchers are skeptical and conservative about using this methodology to reward or punish teachers is that teachers' performance as measured by value-added models can fluctuate sharply over time and can be unevenly distributed across districts (Viadero, 2008a). Some research findings illustrate this complexity. For example, for the issue of uneven geographic distribution, researchers who used the value-added methodology to rank teachers in seven large Florida school districts found that the proportion of teachers who stayed in the top quintile on average in all seven districts, as measured by student gain scores on state assessments from one year to the next, ranged from about a quarter in one district to about a half in another. As to the issue of fluctuation, selected research findings characterized correlations in the percentage of teachers who stayed in the same quintile from one year to the next as "moderate" (Viadero, 2008a). Other researchers, notably Sanders and Horn (1994), found that estimates of school and teacher effects tended to be consistent from year to year. What is clear is that using the value-added data across multiple years is a safer approach to applying the findings to teacher effectiveness.

Another frequently noted problem with value-added methods is that they operate on several assumptions that may not be plausible in the real world. Some value-added models (in particular, Sanders' EVAAS model) are based on the rationale that students serve as their own "control" or "blocking factor." The progress made by students is evaluated relative to their own prior achievement, so as to filter the confounding influences exerted by exogenous factors and, thus, allow for an exclusive examination on the effect of the school and teachers (Sanders & Horn, 1994). However, the statistical "blocking" adjustment is contingent on the condition that there is a careful, systematically balanced assignment of students to teachers (Kupermintz, 2003). Results might be biased if it turns out that a school's students are not randomly assigned to teachers; for example, if principals routinely give high-achieving students to the teachers who are considered the school's best (Viadero, 2008a). Rothstein (2009) articulated this problem by stating "classroom assignments respond dynamically to annual achievement in ways that are not captured by controls typically included in VAM specification" (p. 3).

Another reason that we should be cautious about using VAM is that teachers appear not to be similarly effective with students of different ability levels. For instance, a study by researchers from the RAND Corporation found that the heterogeneity of student ability accounts for approximately 2 to 4 percent of the classroom-to-classroom variations in teachers' effects on student achievement. Although the effects are small, Lockwood stated that "if you give teachers a different group of kids, they would've still gotten answers that differed, but not by a lot," (Lockwood as cited in Viadero, 2008a, p. 13). Kupermintz (2003) corroborated this viewpoint: "[E]qually competent teachers will produce different results with groups of students that differ appreciably in cognitive, affective, and motivational aptitude profiles" (p. 291).

Offering conflicting findings on the matter of reliability of VAM findings, Mendro et al. (1998a) found that teacher effectiveness was remarkably consistent regarding the fact "that teachers have large effects on student achievement, that the measures of effectiveness are stable over time..." (p. 1). Sanders and Rivers (1996) found effective teachers are effective with students with all achievement levels, and oppositely, ineffective teachers are ineffective with all students regardless of performance levels. Consistent with these findings, Aaronson, Barrow, and Sander (2007) estimated that teacher effects are relatively stable over time, reasonably impervious to a variety of conditioning variables, and do not appear to be driven by classroom sorting (i.e., student/teacher assignment) or selective use of test scores (p. 97). In summary, the empirical studies to date are somewhat inconsistent regarding the magnitude of teacher effects, perhaps as a result of the different methodologies and statistical models they implemented.

It is challenging to disentangle a teacher's contribution from the influence of preexisting student differences. Student characteristics or socioeconomic backgrounds might not only account for the variability in their academic achievement, but also for the variability in their pace of making progress. Consequently, VAM cannot answer with complete precision the degree to which achievement gains are attributed to students, teachers, or other factors.

EVAAS, probably the most sophisticated value-added model currently in use, must address a number of significant issues before widespread practical adoption. Those issues include an insufficiency of validity studies, a lack of user-friendliness, the methodological problems with missing data, regression to the mean, and a lack of in-depth examination on the impact of student background variables (Amrein-Beardsley, 2008; Viadero, 2008b). Relatedly, another reason that we should be cautious when using VAM findings relates to missing test-score data, an issue with all standardized assessment systems. Missing data can pose difficulties with value-added models because they rely on longitudinal data from several school years (Viadero, 2008a).

A final issue to consider are the data sources used in VAM. VAM heavily depends on student scores on standardized achievement tests. The quality of data entered in the model directly determines the quality of results of the model. How accurately or validly states' criterion-referenced tests can measure student academic growth is still a heatedly debated issue. Furthermore, using student test score gains as the single criterion to judge the performance of teachers oversimplifies the construct of teacher effectiveness (Amrein-Beardsley, 2008). A study by Lockwood and his research team found that teacher effect on student mathematics learning as estimated by VAM is capricious and sensitive to different measures of mathematics achievement. A teacher who is effective in helping students make progress on mathematical problem solving may not necessarily be equally effective in helping students achieve more on mathematical procedures. They also found the variation within teachers across different achievement measures is larger than between-teacher variation (Lockwood, et al., 2007). This study further verifies how complex a construct teacher effectiveness is.

Summary: Value-Added Methodology

Using value-added analysis on student achievement data to measure teacher effectiveness, although imperfect, is still quite promising compared with traditional proxies (i.e., certification, degree, experience) for effectiveness. VAM can be most useful in identifying which teacher is highly effective and which is highly ineffective. However, it functions less well in distinguishing between the vast majority of teachers clustered in the middle (Gordon, Kane, & Staiger, 2006). Additionally, it cannot specify what makes a teacher effective or ineffective. Consequently, more information regarding the directions of professional improvement, multiple sources of data on teacher performance are needed.

Selected Annotated Bibliography

Aaronson, D., Barrow, L., & Sander, W. (2007). Teachers and student achievement in the Chicago public high schools. *Journal of Labor Economics, 25*(1), 95–135.

Overview

In this study, the authors used administrative data from the Chicago public high schools to estimate the importance of teachers on student mathematics test score gains and then related the measures of individual teacher effectiveness to observable characteristics of the instructors.

Methods

Value-added study. Matched student-teacher administrative data were used, which included all students enrolled and teachers working in 88 Chicago high schools from 1996–97 to 1998–99. The study concentrated on ninth grade. In this study, the measure of teacher quality is defined as the effect on ninth-grade math scores of a semester by the instruction with a given teacher, while controlling for prior achievement (i.e., eighth-grade math scores) and student characteristics.

Statistical Analysis

Generalized least squares (GLS).

Key Findings

♦ The dispersion of teacher quality is wide and educationally significant. Controlling for sampling error, a one standard deviation, one semester improvement in math teacher quality raises student math scores by 0.13 grade equivalents. Thus, over two semesters, "a one standard deviation improvement in math teacher quality translates into an increase in math achievement equal to 22% of the average annual gain." (p. 97)

♦ Estimates of teacher effects are relatively stable over time. The estimates are insensitive to a variety of conditioning variables (for instance, type of statistical modeling). Additionally, they do not appear to be affected by classroom sorting (i.e., student/teacher assignment) or selective use of test scores.

♦ While examining teacher effects by students' prior achievement, race and sex, the findings demonstrated that the biggest impact of a higher quality teacher is among African American students. There is no difference between boys and girls.

• A one standard deviation increase in teacher quality of one semester can translate into 23 percent of the average student annual test score gain for African American students (0.20 grade equivalents) and 11 percent of the average annual gain for Hispanic students (0.13 grade equivalents). The impact of having a higher quality teacher is less important for non-African American, non-Hispanic students.

• A one standard deviation increase in teacher quality of one semester can translate into 15 to 16 percent of the average annual test score gain for both boys and girls.

• Value-added estimates of teacher quality are not correlated to student initial test scores. That means an effective teacher performs well among both low- and high-ability students, whereas an ineffective teacher is ineffective with both types of students.

♦ The vast majority of the variation in teacher effects is unexplained by easily observable teacher characteristics, including those used in traditional human capital measures for determining compensation.

• While some teacher attributes are consistently related to the teacher quality measure, together they explain at most 10 percent of the total variation in estimated teacher quality (p. 97).

- *Years of experience:* Teacher effectiveness may increase slightly (approximately 0.02 grade equivalents) over the first few years of experience, but the impact of years of experience flattens and eventually recedes.

- Teacher gender and race: Female teachers are associated with student test scores approximately 0.07 grade equivalents higher than male teachers, and African American teachers are associated with test scores roughly 0.05 grade equivalents higher than white teachers. Specifically, African American girls and boys tend to have better test score performance when in a classroom with a female teacher (an increase of 0.066 and 0.032 grade equivalents, respectively), or when in a classroom with an African American teacher (an increase of 0.076 and 0.042 grade equivalents, respectively). Considering that the standard errors exist in the statistical analysis, the impact of teacher gender and race on student achievement is minimally small.

- The variables used to determine compensation in Chicago—tenure, advanced degrees, and teaching certification—explain roughly 1 percent of the total variation in estimated teacher quality.

Allington, R. L., & Johnston, P. H. (2000). *What do we know about effective fourth-grade teachers and their classrooms?* **Albany, NY: The National Research Center on English Leaning & Achievement, State University of New York.**

Overview

The conventional process-product research designs pit one teaching strategy against another, thus assuming that it is certain instructional interventions that matter for student learning. However, the issue that arises time after time is the certainty that what really matters is how teachers implement and adapt particular instructional methods and materials to their own teaching settings. There is a need for research to focus on a deeper understanding about the complexities of classroom life. An examination of exemplary teachers regarding how they adjust instruction to maximize student learning can generate new knowledge about teacher effectiveness.

Methods

The authors reviewed available research on exemplary literacy teaching at the upper-elementary grade levels and then summarized selected the features associated with effective teaching as reflected in the literature. Additionally, the authors observed and interviewed thirty fourth-grade teachers in twenty-four schools in five states, who were identified as exemplary through a snowball nomination process (people were asked to nominate the teachers in whose classroom they would place their own children). Then they compared the study results of the nature of classroom talk, curriculum materials, organization of instruction, and evaluation in exemplary teaching with previous studies, revealing a substantial convergence between them.

Key Findings

- ◆ A post hoc analysis of achievement test gains indicated that the gains made by students taught by exemplary teachers outpaced expected levels of growth.

- ◆ The exemplary teachers produce the kinds of student literacy achievement that is beyond even the most sophisticated standardized tests. That means the student achievement growth (either intellectual development or social development) and the conception of exemplary teaching cannot be fully captured by standardized test scores.

- ◆ The exemplary fourth-grade literacy teachers exhibited the following features:

  - The nature of classroom talk

    - Classroom talk could be described as respectful, supportive, and productive and was not only modeled by the teacher in interactions with students, but also deliberately taught and expected.

    - The talk between teacher and students was personalized and personal. Exemplary teachers used authentic conversation to learn about students. Also, they encouraged students to engage each other's ideas. The authority to engage in conversation was more distributed than centralized.

    - Rarely were the words, "no" or "yes," uttered by the teachers except in response to gross social transgression.

    - The classroom talk made genuine inquiry possible, and inquiry processes a normal topic of conversation.

  - Curriculum materials

- Instruction was multisourced. The exemplary teachers were inclined to stretch reading and writing beyond the textbooks.

- A strong literary emphasis pervaded the classrooms, including use of tradebooks in content areas to model thinking and composing strategies as well as to promote a "just reading" framework.

• Organization of instruction

- The exemplary teachers were planful, but at the same time, prepared to capitalize on open instructional opportunities.

- They strategically arranged for students to have choices, and to make them productively, or learn from their errors.

- They were more often observed to work alongside students, individually or in small groups, than work from the front of the room.

- Tailored, collaborative, meaningful problem solving work dominated the instruction.

• The nature of evaluation

- The students were more likely to be evaluated based on improvement, progress, and efforts than on the achievement of a single *a priori* standard.

Ballou, D., Sanders, W., & Wright, P. (2004). Controlling for student background in value-added assessment of teachers. *Journal of Educational and Behavioral Statistics, 29(1),* 37–65,

Overview

The Tennessee Value-Added Assessment System (TVAAS) measures teacher effectiveness on the basis of student gains. Student initial level of achievement is measured by pretest scores, and the contribution of schools and teachers to student progress is identified with the residual differences in students posttest scores of the same achievement scale. Because the value-added method measures gain from a student's own starting point and students can serve as their own blocking factors, it implicitly controls for socioeconomic status and other background factors whose influence on posttest is already reflected in the pretest score. However, the absence of explicit controls for student background has been criticized on the grounds that these factors not only influence the starting point but also the rate at which a student learns (i.e., gain).

Methods

In this research, the authors modified the TVAAS by introducing student socioeconomic status and demographics and using conventional statistical tests to ascertain whether they matter. The authors first removed the influence of teacher quality by estimating the effect of socioeconomic status and demographics in a model with teacher fixed effects. Then they removed the influence of socioeconomic status and demographic factors from student test scores, using the residual scores as dependent variables in the TVAAS.

Concerns About TVAAS

- There is no assurance that students and teachers are randomly assigned to schools/classroom. If better teachers tend to teach in schools or classrooms serving more affluent students, or if more affluent parents seek to enroll them children in the schools or classrooms staffed with better teachers, or if disadvantaged students are systematically assigned to less effective schools and teachers, then demographics and socioeconomic status would become proxies for teacher and school quality. Therefore, the inclusion of socioeconomic status in TVAAS as a control can confound genuine differences in school and teacher quality. The purpose of this study was to examine if that is true.

- This research did not resolve all questions about the TVAAS. TVAAS may not be able to control for other contextual variables (e.g., peer influences) in the same way as it controls the influence of socioeconomic status and demographics.

Key Findings

- The inclusion of controls (e.g., socioeconomic status, race, gender) at the student level has negligible impact on the estimated teacher effects generated by TVAAS, even for teachers whose classes are entirely poor or entirely minority. For all subjects and grades, the correlation between initial teacher effects and those obtained after the inclusion of these controls exceeds 0.90. The adjusted and unadjusted models agree far more than they disagree on the identity of the teachers who are significantly above or below average.

- Four possible explanations for these findings were provided:

- The socioeconomic makeup of students is fairly even across teachers. The variation of socioeconomic status is insufficient to confound teachers' effects, even if it matters.

- Even when there is certain variability in the demographic makeup across teachers, the impact of socioeconomic status and demographics on achievement growth is still ignorable.

- Student demographics do matter, but their impact was not revealed by the statistical analysis as a result of statistical deficiencies such as shrinkage.

- Socioeconomic status and demographic covariates add little information beyond that contained in the covariance of test scores.

Bembry, K. L., Jordan, H. R., Gomez, E., Anderson, M. C., & Mendro, R. L. (1998, April). *Policy implications of long-term teacher effects on student achievement.* **Paper presented at the 1998 Annual Meeting of the American Educational Research Association, San Diego, CA.**

Overview

This paper discusses the policy implications of value-added research on the longitudinal teacher effects on student achievement. The research shows that teachers have a long-term impact on student achievement and that teacher effectiveness is largely impervious to typical approaches of intervention. The paper considers the implications of these results on an array of educational issues, such as student equity, teacher staff development, teacher class assignment, teacher appraisal, curriculum, and administration training and performance.

Methods

This study used longitudinal research design, which involved complicated statistical controlling. The data sources include the three- or four-year reading and math scores of approximately 29,500 students and the teacher effectiveness values of more than 2,000 teachers.

Statistical Analysis

A two-stage, two-level regression/hierarchical linear modeling (HLM) was used. All subgroups were first analyzed with an analysis of covariance using the pretest scores as the covariate, the effectiveness level of the teacher for each year as a blocking variable to form three or four analysis groups, and the three or four years of test scores as the dependent variable.

Research Method Concerns

- ♦ There was statistically significant interaction among the levels of three or four analysis groups.

- ♦ The tests of regression slopes between analysis groups showed significant differences in slopes between the groups in most of the analyses.

- ♦ Large differences in the size of some subgroups existed.

The authors defended the study in that even though there are statistically significant differences in the above-mentioned issues, they are not practically significant because of the large sample size.

Key Findings

- ♦ General results of the research on teacher effectiveness

  - Teachers have significant effects on student achievement, and those effects (either positive or negative) are strongly accumulative over time.

  - It is a false assumption that assigning a highly effective teacher to students who have had an ineffective teacher can make up the difference. Even three years of time cannot remedy entirely the loss of achievement.

  - Teacher effectiveness remains relatively stable over time and largely immutable to typical approaches to change. The major effect of principals in changing school effectiveness is achieved by changing staff members.

  - Students who were assigned to higher-quality teachers tended to have better learning outcomes.

- ♦ The characteristics shared commonly by the top elementary math teachers include:

  - They are knowledgeable about their subject content and are able to provide clear, in-depth explanation to students.

  - They cover thoroughly the entire curriculum and particularly the higher-order skills and concepts.

  - They assess students regularly through multiple means.

  - They provide deep instruction and engage students in deep learning.

- ♦ The implications for the policies related to student equity

- Bias analysis indicated that students with low achievement tend to be assigned to less-effective teachers and students with high achievement tend to be assigned to more-effective teachers.

- All students deserve quality education, but equal access to quality education is jeopardized for students who are assigned to a less-effective teacher.

- Uneven distribution of quality teachers is not a random or occasional occurrence, but a systemic bias.

- It is the school's responsibility to remediate students who are already affected by less-than-effective teachers and to eliminate systemic bias in student–teacher assignment.

Goldhaber, D. D., & Brewer, D. J. (1997). Why don't schools and teachers seem to matter? Assessing the impact of unobservables on educational productivity. *The Journal of Human Resources, 32*(3), 505–523.

Overview

The purpose of this paper was to use a variety of models to investigate the impact of observable and unobservable school-level characteristics on student outcomes.

Some examples of observable variables include class sizes; teacher experience and education; expenditures per pupil; teacher degree level; and teacher undergraduate/graduate degree.

Some examples of unobservable variables include teacher skill; behavior; motivation; and classroom peer effects.

Methods

This study used student data on both eighth and tenth grade math achievement tests, drawn from the *National Educational Longitudinal Study of 1988* (NELS:88), which allowed linking students to specific teachers and classes.

The authors used four statistical models to analyze data.

Findings

- Model 1: Standard ordinary least squares (OLS) educational production functions

  - Dependent Variable: Tenth-grade mathematics test scores

- Independent Variable 1: Student individual and family background variables (including sex, race/ethnicity, parental education, family structure, family income, and eighth-grade math test score)

- Independent Variable 2: School variables (including urbanicity and regional dummies, school size, the percentage of students at the school who are from single-parent families, and the percentage of teachers at the school with at least a master's degree)

- Independent Variable 3: Teacher characteristics (including sex, race/ethnicity, years of experience at the secondary level, and whether the teacher is certified in mathematics, the teacher's degree level, and whether the teacher's B.A. or M.A. major is in math)

- Independent Variable 4: Classroom variables (including class sizes and percentage of minority students)

- Findings:

  - Individual and family background variables alone explained roughly three-quarters of the variance in the student test score performance on ninth-grade math. The impact is mostly attributable to student eighth-grade test scores, i.e., student prior achievement.

  - The school variables jointly have a significant correlation with student achievement, but individually there coefficients are quite small.

  - The teacher variables jointly have a significant correlation with student achievement. Specifically, students taught by more experienced teachers attained higher scores; female teachers are associated with higher student test scores; and black teachers are associated with lower student test scores. In addition, a teacher holding a master's degree is negatively associated with student achievement, though not statistically significant, and teacher certification is negatively associated with test scores, with a statistical significance. However, math-specific degree and certification are found to have significantly positive impact on student achievement.

- Model 2: Adding "teacher behavior" variables (unobservable variables) to Model 1

- Independent Variable: Teacher behavior, which is assessed by: (1) the percentage of the teacher's time in class devoted to small groups and individualized instruction; (2) the percentage of time maintaining order and doing administrative tasks; (3) whether the teacher uses oral questions frequently and emphasizes problem solving; (4) whether the teacher has no control over curriculum content; (5) teaching technique and disciplinary policy; and (6) whether the teacher feels well prepared.
- Findings:
  - The new model with teacher behavior variables is marginally better at explaining variance in student test scores than the first model which only includes teacher characteristics.
  - There is no strong interaction/relationship between teacher characteristics and teacher behavior variables. This means the inclusion of unobservables would not change the estimates of observable school-level variables.
  - Teachers who have little control or no control over their teaching technique are associated with lower student test scores.
  - Teachers who teach in smaller groups and emphasize problem solving are also associated with lower student math scores. (This finding does not necessarily mean that those techniques are detrimental to student learning. They simply may not be effective in improving student performance on conventional standardized tests.)
- Model 3: School and teacher random-effects and fixed-effects models
  - Findings: Unobservable school, teacher, and class characteristics are important in explaining student achievement but do not appear to be correlated with observable variables. (p. 519)
- Model 4: Auxiliary models using estimated fixed effects
  - Findings: The auxiliary regression results confirmed the earlier findings regarding the importance of teacher characteristics: teacher math-specific certification, experience, and math-specific degrees are all statistically significant and positive.

Hanushek, E. A., Kain, J. F., & Rivkin, S. G. (1998, August). *Teachers, schools, and academic achievement.* Cambridge, MA: National Bureau of Economic Research. Retrieved January 24, 2009, from http://www.nber.org/papers/w6691.

Overview

The authors identified four basic questions underlying the policy debate on the role of schools in producing achievement: (1) Do schools "make a difference" or not? (Or are there significant differences among schools in their ability to raise achievement?); (2) If so, what are the sources for such differences? The teachers? The principals? Or the organization of the schools? (3) Are the differences of school overall effects systematically related to school resources or to measurable aspects of schools and teachers? (4) Is the impact of any systematic differences in resources sufficient to justify policy initiatives designed to provide more of those resources? (pp. 1–2) Those are also the research questions addressed in this study.

Methods

This study used a large sample of data and disentangled the separate factors influencing achievement with special attention given to the role of teacher differences and other aspects of schools.

Unique matched panel data on student achievement from the Harvard/UTD Texas School Project (more than 200,000 students in more than 3,000 schools in Texas) permitted identification of both total effects and the impact of specific, measured components of teachers and schools. Panel data is a type of data that can implicitly control for the time invariant individual and school effects on achievement.

Statistical Analysis

♦ Value-added regression.

Key Findings

♦ There are large differences among schools in their impact on student achievement. The *between-school variance* accounts for 5.5 percent and 3.3 percent of the variance in math and reading achievement, respectively, while the *between-school-and-grade variance* accounts for 15.3 percent and 8.9 percent of variance in math and reading achievement. That means there are substantial within-school differences.

   • *Implications:* Schools do make a difference. School quality matters importantly for student academic performance and is an important lever for raising the achievement of low income students to ensure educational equality.

♦ Resource differences explain at most a small part of the difference in school quality. School differences appear to derive most importantly from variations in teacher quality, rather than the overall school organization, leadership, or financial conditions.

  • *Implications:* Heterogeneity among teachers is the most significant source of achievement variations. Additional expenditures or other simplistic resources input may not substantially raise achievement.

♦ Lower bound estimates suggest that variations in teacher quality account for at least 7.5 percent of the total variation in measured achievement gains, and there are reasons to believe that the true percentage is considerably larger.

♦ The differences among teachers cannot be directly measured by observable characteristics of the teachers and classrooms.

♦ Initial years of teaching experience is important in improving a teacher's impact on learning. Specifically, the first and, to a lesser extent, the second years of experience significantly improve teacher quality, but the impact of additional years levels off and is rarely significant.

  • *Implications:* This result implies that initial years of teaching have a negative impact on student achievement. Students who are assigned with new teachers (with one or two years of teaching experience) are in a disadvantaged position compared with the peers who are taught by teachers with three-plus years of service experience.

♦ A postgraduate education or degree is not associated with quality of teaching. The effects of a master's degree are generally negative, although statistically insignificant from zero.

♦ The effects of teaching experience explain only a small amount of the total observed variation in teacher quality.

♦ The evidence on class size is somewhat mixed: class size is negatively associated with math and reading achievement in fourth and fifth grade, but not in sixth grade; smaller class sizes have more positive effect for low-income students in earlier grades.

♦ Class size explains less than 0.1 percent of the total variation in student achievement gains. The contribution of class size to the student achievement is less than one-twentieth of the contribution of teacher quality differences.

Hattie, J. (2003). *Teachers make a difference: What is the research evidence?* **Retrieved December 12, 2008, from http://www.leadspace. govt.nz/leadership/pdf/john_hattie.pdf.**

Overview

Based on an extensive review of literature, the author proposed six major sources that can account for the variance in students' academic achievement (while ignoring their interactions):

- ◆ Students: accounting for approximately 50 percent of the variance of achievement.

- ◆ Home: accounting for approximately 5 to 10 percent of the variance.

- ◆ Schools: accounting for approximately 5 to 10 percent of the variance.

- ◆ Principals: whose influence is already accounted for under the "Schools" category.

- ◆ Peer effects: accounting for approximately 5 to 10 percent of the variance.

- ◆ Teachers: accounting for approximately 30 percent of the variance.

Key Findings

In the author's synthesis of the literature that distinguishes expert teachers from experienced teachers, he constructed five major dimensions and sixteen attributes that can underpin the *expertise* of the expert teachers.

- ◆ Can effectively deliver the content of their subject(s)

  - • Expert teachers represent the content knowledge in a deep and integrated manner.

  - • Expert teachers adopt a problem-solving stance and are flexible enough to take advantage of emerging opportunities while planning and teaching.

  - • Expert teachers are adept at anticipating problems, dedicating planning time to develop strategies to address those problems, and improvising as required by the situation.

- Expert teachers are better decision-makers and can maintain a balance between content-centered and student-centered instruction.

♦ Guiding Learning through classroom interactions

- Expert teachers are proficient at creating a learning climate that is optimal for learning.

- Expert teachers have a keen perception of the multidimensional complexities of classroom situations and are able to modify their instructional based on their observation.

- Expert teachers make instruction decisions based on contextual factors, e.g., student ability, background, and surrounding settings.

♦ Monitoring learning and providing feedback

- Expert teachers are more skilled at monitoring student learning and assessing their level of understanding and progress, and, importantly, they provide much relevant, useful feedback that is responsive to individuals.

- Expert teachers are adept at developing and testing hypotheses about learning difficulties or instructional strategies.

- Expert teachers are more automatic with their cognition and behavior, freeing their working memory to deal with complex classroom situation.

♦ Holding positive affective attributes toward teaching and learning

- Expert teachers are respectful to and caring of the students.

- Expert teachers are enthusiastic about teaching and learning.

♦ Improving student educational outcomes

- Expert teachers increase students' responsibility and sense of ownership regarding their learning, by developing their self-regulation skills, involving them in mastery learning and enhancing their self-efficacy and self-esteem as learners.

- Expert teachers provide tasks and goals that are challenging to but attainable by students.

- Expert teachers positively influence students' learning outcomes.

- Expert teachers keep a balance between surface learning and deep learning so as to optimize student achievement in both content and higher-order skills.

Heistad, D. (1999). *Teachers who beat the odds: Value-added reading instruction in Minneapolis 2nd grade.* **Paper presented at the Annual American Educational Research Association Conference, April, Montreal, Canada.**

Overview

Prior studies on teacher effects in reading have used models that failed to fully account for student background differences and prior reading ability. This study used data from four successive school years to (1) establish a measure of teacher effectiveness in improving reading achievement, (2) explore the stability of teacher effects in reading cross years, and (3) investigate teachers' behaviors that correlate with teacher effects. Stability/consistency is essential for valid teacher quality indicators, because only after the stability of teacher effectiveness has been established and the effects of time invariant within classroom factors controlled can the measurement of teacher quality be used for teacher accountability or other high-stakes decisions.

Methods

A value-added model was used to isolate teacher effects from the effects of student characteristics such as race, poverty, gender, family composition, prior achievement, and special learning needs.

Instrument

California Achievement Tests were used to measure reading comprehension achievement.

A three-part teacher survey to assess reading instruction strategies, general philosophy of reading instruction, and use of test preparation activities also was used.

Research Method Concerns

- The value-added model used in this study assumed there is no interaction between teacher effects and student demographic characteristics. It also assumed no interaction among teacher effects for students instructed by more than one teacher.

- The particular measurement instrument in this study may not reflect all relevant aspects of second grade reading.

♦ The value-added coefficient estimated in this study is limited by the available student and family characteristic variable coded in the district center computer system. This coefficient may be biased due to missing student demographics, school characteristics, or neighborhood variables (for example, family income, parent education level).

Key Findings

♦ In the preliminary tests of the study, student characteristics (e.g., gender, prior achievement, poverty, race, English proficiency, special education status, neighborhood poverty) have contributed to the prediction of second grade reading proficiency.

♦ Teacher effects account for 4.3 percent to 9.2 percent of the variance in student pre-/posttest scores.

♦ Teacher effects in second grade reading were found to have moderate stability over two successive years with median correlations varying from 0.4 to 0.6 depending on the number of students with pre- and posttest scores in a classroom. Estimates of teacher effect stability increased substantially when value-added effects were aggregated over three or more years.

♦ No significant correlation was found between value-added teacher effects and teacher years of experience.

♦ No significant correlation was found between value-added teacher effects and teacher credits earned.

♦ Based on the results of a self-report survey, several facets of direct instruction philosophy and practice correlated dependably with teacher effects. Teachers who demonstrated the high value-added effects tended to:

• Disagree with the notion that reading and writing develop naturally, like speaking;

• Use more small group instruction;

• Use more teacher-directed instruction and guided practice that student choice;

• Use more development of word attack strategies;

• Use more individual student oral reading;

• Use more systematic motivational strategies;

- Use test preparation activity and published test preparation materials.

Jordan, H. R., Mendro, R. L., & Weerasinghe, D. (1997, July). *Teacher effect on longitudinal student achievement.* **Paper presented at the CREATE Annual Meeting, Indianapolis, IN.**

Overview

The Tennessee Value-Added Assessment System (TVAAS) has been used to obtain teacher effects on student achievement by eliminating effects of factors that reside outside the control of the teacher and school. Regarding the validity of this system, certain researchers criticize that the teacher effects identified by the system are unrelated to students' real level of achievement and that these effects are statistical artifacts. In response to this criticism, the authors used the Dallas Public Schools' assessment model to investigate the longitudinal teacher effects on student achievement in reading and mathematics. The purpose of this study was to determine whether the findings generated by TVAAS (i.e., teacher effectiveness is the dominant factor affecting student academic achievement) are generalizable to (1) a different methodological approach, (2) a different population of students, (3) a different measure of student academic achievement, and (4) different cohorts of a student population. The findings of this study generally support former research by showing that teacher effectiveness is strongly related to student outcomes.

Methods

A two-stage regression/hierarchical linear model (HLM) was used to analyze student achievement data on reading and mathematics from fourth grade to eighth grade in Dallas schools system. The Dallas Classroom Effectiveness Indices were calculated to produce estimates of teacher effectiveness levels of teachers.

Key Findings

- ◆ Teacher effectiveness is strongly related to student outcomes as indicated in the following findings:
  - Students with no Quintile 1 (least-effective) teacher would have a 7 in 10 chance of being in the top half of effect size distribution.
  - Students with no Quintile 5 (most-effective) teacher would have a 2 in 3 chance of being in the bottom half of effect size distribution.

- With no Quintile 1 teacher, students have less than a 1 in 10 chance of being in the bottom 20 percent of effect size distribution.

- With no Quintile 5 teacher, students have less than a 1 in 6 chance of being in the top 20 percent of effect size distribution.

♦ Value-added assessment can efficiently identify the teachers in any year whose effect on student learning is detrimental or beneficial.

♦ The results of value-added analysis on student achievement in relation to teacher quality have important implications for teacher appraisal and professional development programs.

Leigh, A. (n.d.). *Estimating teacher effectiveness from two-year changes in students' test scores.* **Retrieved May 22, 2007, from http://econrsss.anu.edu.au/~aleigh/.**

Overview

Most professional areas have a straightforward and transparent evaluation system, although in the profession of teaching, it is much trickier to determine who is effective and who is not. Because student scores on achievement scales are positively correlated with educational and labor force outcomes, they should be the valid benchmark for evaluating teacher effectiveness. However, the barrier is that student scores are not just subject to teacher effects alone; they also are impacted by family background and many other factors. In this paper, the author addressed this issue by using student panel data.

Methods

The author used a database that covered more than 10,000 Australian primary school teachers and more than 90,000 pupils to estimate teacher effectiveness. Teacher output/teacher effectiveness is measured by the score gains made by the students they taught in a second standardized test, as compared to the first test which took place two years earlier.

Statistical Analysis

Fixed effects regression.

Key Findings

♦ Teachers have a significant impact on student achievement gains. After adjusting for measurement error, the teacher fixed effects are widely dispersed across teachers.

- Having a teacher at the twenty-fifth percentile versus having a teacher at the seventy-fifth percentile would result in a difference of one-seventh of a standard deviation in student scores. Because a 0.5 standard deviation increase in student test scores is equivalent to a full year's learning, this finding can translate to a seventy-fifth percentile teacher achieves in three-quarters of a year what a twenty-fifth percentile teacher achieves in a full year.

- Having a teacher at the tenth percentile versus having a teacher at the ninetieth percentile would raise student test scores by one quarter of a standard deviation. This finding can translate to a ninetieth percentile teacher achieves in half a year what a tenth percentile teacher achieves in a full year.

♦ Teacher fixed effects have significant correlations with certain observable teacher characteristics, but these factors explain very little of the variance among teachers.

- Experience is positively related to student test score gain, but there is a nonlinear relationship between them. For both literacy and numeracy, there is a significant effect of experience in the early years of a teacher's career.

- Female teachers are more proficient in teaching literacy.

- Teachers with a master degree or some other form of further qualification do not achieve significantly larger achievement gains.

- Overall, the combination of qualifications, gender, age, experience, and other identifiable ratings account for less than one-hundredth of the variance in teacher effectiveness. Most of the differences among teachers are a result of factors not captured by the current salary schedules in Australia, which are totally based on experience and qualification. Alternative salary structures should be considered.

- Investment in improving teacher quality could be at least as cost-effective as class-size reduction.

Mendro, R. L., Jordan, H. R., Gomez, E., Anderson, M. C., & Bembry, K. L. (1998, April). *Longitudinal teacher effects on student achievement and their relation to school and project evaluation.* Paper presented at the 1998 Annual Meeting of the American Educational Research Association, San Diego, CA.

Mendro, R. L., Jordan, H. R., Gomez, E., Anderson, M. C., & Bembry, K. L. (1998, April). *An application of multiple linear regression in determining longitudinal teacher effectiveness.* Paper presented at 1998 Annual Meeting of the American Educational Research Association, San Diego, CA.

Overview

These two papers present evidence from an empirical study designed to estimate teacher effectiveness relative to student achievement over a four-year period and to determine the size of the effects. The effects of the teacher on student achievement were found to be pervasive. The effects are of sufficient magnitude that they overwhelm the effects of typical programs and treatments.

Methods

In this longitudinal study student residuals are calculated from a two-stage hierarchical linear modeling (HLM) process to determine school and teacher effectiveness. The first stage uses multiple linear regression to remove the effects of concomitant variables (e.g., gender, ethnicity, socioeconomic status, and language proficiency) and their interactions from student achievement measures. The second stage uses an HLM procedure with the residuals from the first stage to control for school-related variables (e.g., percent minority, average socioeconomic status, percent mobility). Residuals from this model were then matched back to teachers and classrooms. Classroom effectiveness indices were produced from these data. The assessment used to measure the dependent variable—student achievement residual gains—was the Iowa Tests of Basic Skills (ITBS).

Key Findings

♦ The research findings in the study on teacher effectiveness were remarkably consistent regarding the fact "that teachers have large effects on student achievement, that the measures of effectiveness are stable over time, and that the effects teachers have are on an order of magnitude which dwarfs the effects associated with curriculum, staff development, restructuring, and other types of educational interventions" (p. 1).

♦ Ineffective teachers have negative longitudinal effects on student learning. If the students have a less-effective teacher in the first year and the highest level teachers for remaining years, their achievement could never exceed that of the students who have been assigned with effective teachers for all the years. Two years of effective teachers could not remediate the achievement loss caused by one year with a poor teacher. With three years of effective teachers, the students have a 1 in 8 chance of making it back to the top.

♦ Implication for educational evaluation and research: Teachers have a large effect on their students' achievement, of a magnitude that overshadows the effect of a typical educational intervention or experiment. Therefore, when we evaluate an educational intervention or program, the effectiveness level of the teachers in the field must be taken into account, particularly when this evaluation occurs in an environment of intact classrooms and schools where experimental control on teacher effectiveness is not possible.

Munoz, M. A., & Chang, F. C. (2007). The elusive relationship between teacher characteristics and student academic growth: A longitudinal multilevel model for change. *Journal of Personnel Evaluation in Education, 20,* 147–164.

Overview

The literature has been consistent in finding that teachers have an important effect on student learning, but existing empirical studies reached mixed conclusions when it comes to specific teacher characteristics. This study used a longitudinal, value-added approach to evaluate the effects of teacher characteristics (i.e., experience, education, and race) on high school reading achievement gains.

Methods

Longitudinal, hierarchical linear modeling (HLM) model. Sample data for this study came from a large urban school district.

Instrument

PAS ThinkLink benchmark tests as measurements of student achievement.

Research Method Concerns

A key issue to consider is that teacher quality is much larger and much more complicated than just experience, education, and race. There are myriad potential confounding factors that limit the internal and external validity of findings.

Key Findings

♦ Between-classroom variance accounts for approximately 14 percent of total variance in student achievement.

♦ The correlation between student initial achievement status and growth rate is 0.03, which means students' baseline reading achievement was not closely related to their reading growth rate.

♦ None of the teacher variables examined in this study (i.e., experience, education, and race) added to the prediction in students' growth rates of achievement. In other words, teaching experience, education level, and race were not significantly related to their students' growth rates.

♦ The authors proposed two possible reasons to explain the lack of correlation between teacher characteristics and student achievement gains:

• The teacher preparation programs in universities did not prepare teachers adequately to be effective in high-poverty urban settings.

• The teachers did not receive in-service professional development to effectively transfer what they learned into the classroom.

♦ A traditional compensation system that pays teachers based on education and years of experience will not necessarily result in an increase in student learning. Performance-based pay might have a positive impact on students' test scores and may prove cost-effective.

Nye, B., Konstantopoulos, S., & Hedges, L. V. (2004). How large are teacher effects? *Educational Evaluation and Policy Analysis, 26(3), 237–257.*

Methods

Using data from a four-year (kindergarten to grade 3) experiment in which teachers and students were randomly assigned to classes, known as the Tennessee Class Size Experiment or Project STAR (Student–Teacher Achievement Ratio), this study focused on estimating teacher effects on student achievement. The study involved students in seventy-nine elementary schools in forty-two school districts in Tennessee. Within each school, kindergarten students were randomly assigned to classrooms in one of the three treatment conditions: small classes (with thirteen to seventeen students), larger classes (with twenty-two to twenty-six students) or larger classes with a full-time classroom aide. Teachers were also assigned randomly to these types of classes. The hierarchical linear model (HLM) was used to determine the achievement differences among classrooms. That achievement difference equals the teacher effectiveness difference.

Random assignment of students and teachers was considered very important for this study. If the classes within each school are initially equivalent (because of random assignment), then any systematic differences in mean achievement among classes can be attributed to the one of the two resources: the treatment (small classes, larger classes, or larger classes with a full-time aide) or differences in teacher effectiveness. Furthermore, if there is a systematic difference in achievement among classrooms that were assigned to the *same* treatment type within schools, then that differences can be totally attributed to the variance in teacher effectiveness. The results of statistical analysis also confirmed that random assignment was successful in assuring there was no significant difference among students in terms of their socioeconomic status, ethnicity, and age across classrooms, across treatment types, and even across classrooms within the same treatment type. The statistical analysis also found that random assignment is successful in ensuring there is no difference among teachers in terms of their race, experience, and education across treatment types.

Instrument

Stanford Achievement Test (SAT) in reading and mathematics.

Key Findings

♦ The authors conducted a literature synthesis on seventeen previous studies of the magnitude of teacher effects, finding that from 7 to 21 percent of the variance in student achievement gains is associated with variation in teacher effectiveness.

♦ Variance because of differences among teachers is substantial in comparison to the variance between schools. (Within-school variance is much larger than between-school variance.) The effects between-teacher variance is over twice as large as the effects of between-school variance on student grade 2 reading and more than three times as large at grade 3 reading. This suggests that naturally occurring teacher effects are typically larger than naturally occurring school effects. Thus (at least in this study where random assignment is in place), which teacher a student happens to get within a school matters more than which school the student happens to get.

♦ The variance of the teacher effects in mathematics is much larger than that in reading. This may be because mathematics is mostly learned in school and, thus, may be more directly influenced by teachers, or that there is more variation in how (or how well or how much) teachers teach mathematics.

♦ Variation in class sizes cannot explain variance across teachers in student achievement or achievement gains. This means class size cannot explain teacher effects.

♦ Neither teacher experience nor teacher education can explain much variance in teacher effects (never more than 5 percent). The estimated effect of teacher experience on achievement gains was positive in every case except first grade math, where it was negative, at near zero. The magnitude of the estimated positive effects was negligible, ranging from 0.06 to 0.19 standards deviations, but only statistically significant for grade 2 reading and grade 3 mathematics.

♦ The estimated effects of teacher education were generally smaller than those of teacher experience, and were negligible in grades 1 and 3, but were significant for grade 3 mathematics achievement gains with a difference of 0.09 standard deviation.

♦ The between-teacher (but within-school and within-treatment) variance is always larger in low socioeconomic status schools. This means the distribution of teacher effectiveness is much more uneven in low socioeconomic status schools than in high socioeconomic status schools. In addition, the proportion of the total variance in student achievement gains accounted for by the teacher effect is higher in low socioeconomic status schools. This means, in low socioeconomic status schools, it matters more which teacher a child receives than it does in high-socioeconomic status schools.

♦ The variation in student socioeconomic status cannot explain the variance of teacher effectiveness within schools. This means an effective teacher is effective with all students, regardless of the students' socioeconomic status backgrounds, whereas an ineffective teacher is ineffective with all students.

♦ There are substantial differences among teachers in the ability to produce achievement gains in their students. If teacher effects are normally distributed,

  • the difference in student achievement gains between having a twenty-fifth percentile teacher (a not-so-effective teacher) and a seventy-fifth percentile teacher (an effective teacher) is more than one-third of a standard deviation (0.35) in reading and almost half a standard deviation (0.48) in mathematics.

  • the difference in student achievement gains between having a fiftieth percentile teacher (an average teacher) and a ninetieth percentile teacher (a very effective teacher) is about one-third of a standard deviation (0.33) in reading and somewhat smaller than half a standard deviation (0.46) in mathematics.

  • in kindergarten the effects are comparable, but somewhat larger for reading.

♦ Because teacher effects are found to be larger than school effects, educational policies focusing on teacher effects as the main determinant of student achievement will be more promising than policies focusing on school effects.

♦ The effect of one standard deviation change in teacher effectiveness is larger than that of reducing class size from twenty-five to fifteen.

Summary

It is widely accepted that teachers differ in their effectiveness, yet the empirical evidence regarding teacher effectiveness is weak. The authors used data from a four-year experiment in which teachers and students were randomly assigned to classes to estimate teacher effects on student achievement. Larger teacher effects were found on mathematics achievement than on reading achievement. The estimated relationship of teacher experience with student achievement gains is statistically significant only for second-grade reading and third-grade mathematics achievement. Much larger teacher effect variance was found in low socioeconomic status schools than in high socioeconomic status schools.

Odden, A., Borman, G., & Fermanich, M. (2004). Assessing teacher, classroom, and school effects, including fiscal effects. *Peabody Journal of Education, 79*(4), 4–32.

Overview

Improvement of student learning is recognized to emerge from three different arenas of the educational system: the student, the classroom, and the school (p. 5). Previous research tended to assess the effects of student, classroom, and school variables in isolation from other variables and has often used statistical techniques that ignored the nested nature of the three classes of factors. This study looked into a more educationally oriented framework to assess the effects of these three factors on student learning, particularly student learning gains. The authors suggested that hierarchical linear models (HLMs) can account for the nested nature of the variables and analyze them in a multilevel model, thus, producing more accurate estimates of the magnitude of their effects on student learning.

Methods

Literature review (thematic organization of extant literature).

Key Findings

- ◆ What does research say about teacher and classroom effects?
  - Between-teacher variation of effectiveness is the single largest factor affecting academic growth of populations of students.
  - A school's effect could be largely explained by the aggregation of individual effects of its teachers.
  - Differences in student achievement between classrooms within schools are larger than the differences between schools. The impact that teachers have on student test scores changes is more than twice the impact of the schools.
  - Students learn different amount of content knowledge during a normal academic year.
  - Teacher effects are stable over year. Teachers produce consistently low, medium, or high learning gains year after year.
  - Three categories of factors can account for teachers' impact on student learning:
    - ▪ Teacher characteristics

- ◆ Teachers' degrees and education units beyond a bachelor's degree rarely have an impact on student learning.

- ◆ Years of experience generally have little impact but teachers with three or more years of experience generally are more effective than less-experienced teachers.

- ◆ Previous studies generated mixed findings regarding the effects of teacher licensure.

- ◆ A math-specific college major and courses taken have positive effects on student mathematics learning.

- Teacher classroom practices

  - ◆ Both content coverage and cognitive demands in classroom instruction matter.

  - ◆ Alignment among instruction (e.g., content coverage and cognitive demands) and assessment matters for student test score performance.

  - ◆ Certain teaching practices (e.g., authentic learning, anticipatory set, direct instruction, wait time, time on task, homework) lead to larger learning gains.

  - ◆ Minority students benefit more from reductions in class size.

  - ◆ Teachers' beliefs, expectations, and behaviors affect African American students more than white students.

- Context

  - ◆ High concentration of poor and minority students can pose a barrier for student learning gains.

◆ What does research say about school effects?

- School leadership

  - Principal leadership explains 2 percent to 8 percent of total variation in test scores among schools. Principals influence school success through indirect or mediated means, for instance, through influencing instructional climate.

- Professional community

  - A professional community that has a shared sense of purpose and engage in collaboration and collective reflection could enhance the instructional capacity of schools and increase student achievement.

- School and class size

  - Optimum size for elementary schools is 300 to 500 students, and the optimum size for secondary schools is 600 to 900 students. Small class size (less than twenty students per class) can improve student achievement scores by 0.1 to 0.4 standard deviations depending on grade level. Small class size is particularly beneficial to economically disadvantaged and minority students.

- Fiscal effects

  - School inputs had little small but positive effects on student achievement. On average, school sources can explain 5 to 9 percent of total variation in student achievement.

◆ What does research say about student effects?

- Student-related variables, such as motivation, cognitive engagement in learning, aptitude, expectations, and aspirations, all affect school outcomes. Variables that are related to students, but may not in their control, such as parental education, parental occupational status, family income, and race/ethnicity, also have stratifying effects on student learning.

◆ The authors suggested that hierarchical linear model (HLM) is the appropriate methodology to analyze the effects of students, teachers, and schools, because:

- HLM takes into account the nested nature of data—student level is nested within the classroom level, and classroom level is nested within school level.

- HLM can estimate between- and within-group variance at the same time.

- HLM can make value-added measures of school and teacher performance by isolating statistically schools and teachers effects from other sources of student achievement.

Palardy, G. J., & Rumberger, R. W. (2008). Teacher effectiveness in first grade: The importance of background qualifications, attitudes, and instructional practices for student learning. *Educational Evaluation and Policy Analysis, 30*(2), 111–140.

Overview

Extant research generally reached an agreement that teachers matter for student achievement. However, there is no conclusive answer as to which aspects of teachers matter most. Researchers attempted to address the problem by analyzing two types of teacher data: (1) teachers' professional background characteristics, such as their educational attainment, intelligence test scores, experience, and credentials; and (2) teaching factors—attitudes, beliefs, and teaching practices..

Specifically, this study addressed the following research questions:

♦ What proportion of the variation in student achievement gains can be attributed to each of the three general sources: individual differences between students, classroom effects (including teacher effects), and school effects?

♦ To what degree do differences in teacher effectiveness affect student achievement gains?

♦ What is the relative size of the effect of teachers' background qualifications, attitudes, and instructional practices on student achievement gains in first grade? (pp. 112–113)

Methods

A three-level hierarchical linear model (HLM) was used. Independent variables included teacher background qualifications, attitudes, and instructional practices. Dependent variable was student reading and math achievement gains in first grade.

Findings

♦ Model 1: Unconditional model (which used the student spring achievement test scores as the outcome measures but did not a include covariate, i.e., fall test score, thus no gain score was used in this model)

• Findings: 72.5 percent of the variance in reading achievement and 75.3 percent of the variance in math achievement are attributable to student level; 7.4 percent and 7.9 percent of the variance in reading and math achievement, respectively, are attributable to classroom level; and 20.2 percent of the variance in reading and 18.2 percent of the variance in math are attributable to school level. (Because of the limitations of this model, these estimates are not suitable for making inferences about teacher effectiveness.)

- ◆ Model 2: Residual gain score model (which included fall achievement and assessment gap covariates at the within-classroom level. Gain scores were used.)

  - Findings: The variance in achievement gains at classroom level and at school level was higher for reading than for math: 10.7 percent of reading achievement variance versus 6.8 percent for math achievement variance was at classroom level, and 10.4 percent for reading versus 6.8 percent for math was at school level; and 79.0 percent for reading and 86.4 percent for math was at the student level. This means "there is far more variance in student achievement gains between students within classrooms than between classrooms within schools and between schools" (p.121). "These findings also suggest that there is greater variability in the quality of reading teaching than mathematics teaching in first grade" (p. 121). (This finding is inconsistent with the results of some prior studies.)

- ◆ Model 3: Student model (controlling for individual student socioeconomic status, ethnicity, gender)

  - Findings: Both family socioeconomic status and ethnicity are associated with student achievement gains.

- ◆ Model 4: Classroom composition model (controlling for mean socioeconomic status within classrooms, percentage of minority within classrooms, mean of math scores, mean of reading scores, variance in math scores, variance in reading scores)

  - Findings:

    - Classroom socioeconomic composition, proportion minority, student prior achievement, all are associated with student achievement.

    - In addition to individual student socioeconomic status, the overall classroom socioeconomic status composition also has separate influence on student learning. This composition accounts for an additional 18.1 percent of the classroom variance in reading gains and 7.4 percent of the classroom variation in math gains.

♦ Model 5: Teacher background qualifications model (examining teacher characteristics such as advanced degree, experience, full certification)

  • Findings: Having a full certification (explaining 2.4 percent of the classroom-level variance) was the only teacher background variable that is associated significantly with reading achievement gains, and none was significantly associated with math achievement gains.

♦ Model 6: to investigate the impact of teacher attitudes and practices on achievement gains after controlling for student background, classroom composition, and teacher background

  • Independent variables examined:

    ▪ Teacher attitudes: (1) daily homework; (2) parent supportive; (3) curriculum control; (4) teacher community; (5) teacher efficacy; (6) teacher expectations

    ▪ Teacher instructional practices: (1) amount of time spent on general instruction in reading and math; (2) instructional modalities, including whole-class instruction, small groups, mixed ability groups, peer tutoring, etc.; (3)frequency of use of specific instructional approaches, such as phonics, book projects, math games, etc.

  • Findings:

    ▪ Only one attitude variable, teacher expectations, was found to be significantly associated with reading achievement gains (effect size = −0.04, p <0.05). (p. 124)

    ▪ Reading

      ♦ The general measure, reading instructional frequency, had a significant positive association with reading gains.

      ♦ No measures of instructional modality were significantly associated with reading achievement gains.

      ♦ Five specific measures of instructional practice frequency had significant associations with reading gains: frequency of phonics instruction; frequency of silent reading; frequency of writing from diction, frequency of journal writing, and frequency of letter names.

      ♦ Together, the attitude and practice variables accounted for 14.1 percent of the classroom-level variance in reading achievement gains, nearly six times the effects noted for teacher background.

- Math

  - ◆ Three specific measures of instructional practice frequency had significant associations with math gains: frequency of use of math worksheets, frequency of work on problems with calendar, frequency of use of geometric manipulations.

  - ◆ No measures of instructional time or modality were significantly associated with math achievement gains.

  - ◆ Together, the attitude and practice variables accounted for 8.9 percent of the classroom-level variance in math achievement gains.

◆ How do teachers matter?

- Teachers have a substantial impact on student learning. The effect size of teacher quality is 0.30 for reading and 0.25 for math, after controlling for student characteristics and classroom composition. Although these effect sizes would be deemed as small by conventional standards set in social sciences, they are substantial as compared with other school-related/student-related factors. For example, the effect of teacher for math is approximately five times greater than the effect of family socioeconomic status and more than 2.5 times greater than the effect of a class-size reduction from twenty-five to fifteen students per classroom. Additionally, the teacher quality effect sizes can translate into more than a third (0.38) of a school year of reading achievement gains and one-third (0.33) of a school year for math.

- Teacher background (i.e., the characteristics teacher bring into the classroom) has less robust associations with achievement gains than teacher attitudes and practices (i.e., the attitudes and practices they adopt in the classroom).

- Post hoc analysis indicated that there is little difference in the attitudes and practices of certified teachers compared with noncertified teachers.

- Educational policy should direct more emphasis on improving aspects of teaching, such as instructional practices and teacher attitudes.

♦ Policy implications:

- The "high qualified teacher" provision in NCLB, which screens teachers on the basis of their background qualifications (i.e., degree and certification), is insufficient for ensuring that classrooms will be staffed by teachers who are effective in raising students' achievement.

- The value-added model is suitable for identifying the effectiveness of teachers in raising achievement and could be a valuable evaluation tool to identify under-performing teachers. However, it is less suitable for "providing the type of fine-grained evaluative feedback necessary to promote positive change." "For this reason, improving ineffective teaching will likely require more than value-added assessments but also qualitative reviews of teaching performance once ineffective teachers have been identified as well as structured in-service training and mentoring to ineffective teachers" (p. 129).

Rivkin, S. G., Hanushek, E. A., & Kain, J. F. (2005). Teachers, schools, and academic achievement. *Econometrica, 73*(2), 417–458.

Overview

Since the release of the Coleman Report, there has been a research and policy debate on the issue of the role of schools and teachers in influencing student achievement. This article examined a series of basic questions about the impact of schools and used a panel dataset of students in Texas to identify the sources of differences in student achievement. Specifically, this study disentangled the impact of schools and teachers in influencing student learning, with special attention given to potential problems of contamination from student and school selection or nonrandom teacher assignment practices.

The Coleman Report is frequently interpreted as schools having relatively small effects of differences in attributing to student achievement. In other words, it implies that there are no systematic quality differences among schools and teachers. The study investigated whether schools and teachers make a difference, and if there are significant and systematic differences between schools and teachers in their abilities to raise achievement. If so, can observable characteristics of teachers and schools (e.g., class size, teacher education, and years of teaching experience) account for the quality differences? How large are the effects?

Methods

The authors used an extraordinarily rich dataset that contained test scores spanning grades 3 through 7 for three cohorts of students in the mid-1990s. The mathematics and reading achievement scores of more than 600,000 students from more than 3,000 schools were observed individually, repeatedly and longitudinally.

Key Findings

♦ A substantial share of the overall achievement gain variation occurs between teachers. Teaches have powerful effects on reading and mathematics achievement. Additionally, much of the teacher quality variation exists within rather than between schools.

♦ One standard deviation increase in teacher quality distribution can raises student achievement by at least 0.11 standard deviations in mathematics and 0.095 standard deviations in reading..

♦ High-quality instruction throughout primary school could substantially offset disadvantage associated with a low socioeconomic background.

♦ Little of the variation in teacher quality can be attributed to observable characteristics such as education or experience.

  • There is no evidence that a master's degree raises teacher effectiveness.

  • Experience is not significantly related to achievement following the initial years in the profession. Teacher effectiveness increased during the first year or two but leveled off after the third year. Differences between having a new teacher and having an experienced teacher only account for ten percent of the total teacher quality variance in mathematics and somewhere between five and twenty percent of the variance in reading.

♦ Most teacher effectiveness is a result of unobserved differences in instructional quality.

♦ Class size has small, but significant effects on both mathematics and reading achievement gains in fourth and fifth grade, but the impact declines markedly as students progress through schools and tends to be less significant in reading than in mathematics. The effects of class size are not substantially larger for disadvantaged students.

- The effects of a costly ten-student reduction in class size are smaller than the benefits of moving one standards deviation up the teacher quality distribution.

- Policy implications:

  - Economically disadvantaged students systematically achieve less than their more advantaged peers, on an average of 0.6 standard deviations. Low-income and minority students face higher teacher turnover and tend to be taught more frequently by beginning teachers (p. 450). The estimated variation in the quality of instruction reveals that schools and teachers play an important role in promoting economic and social equality. School policy on teacher quality is an important tool for raising the achievement of low income students. A successive assignment of good teaches can be a big step toward closing achievement gaps cross income groups (p. 449).

  - The drastic quality variation of teachers with similar professional background highlights the importance of more effective practices in hiring, firing, mentoring, and evaluating, and compensating teachers..

Rockoff, J. E. (2004). The impact of individual teachers on student achievement: Evidence from panel data. *The American Economic Review, 94(2), 247–252.*

Overview

The author used a rich set of matched student–teacher panel data to separate student achievement into a series of "fixed effects" and assign importance to students, teachers, schools, and so on, to produce a more accurate estimate of teacher impact on student achievement.

Methods

Value-added research with panel data, which included roughly 10,000 students and 300 teachers.

The virtues of panel data in estimating teacher quality were described as follows:

- Panel data allows the researcher to examine achievement variation of the same student with different teachers and, thus, to distinguish variation in teacher quality from variation in students' cognitive abilities and other characteristics.

- Panel data allows the research to observe the same teacher with multiple classrooms and, thus, to tell differences in teacher quality apart from differences in class size and other classroom-level factors.

- Panel data allow the researcher to focus on variations in student achievement within particular schools and years, thus separating teacher differences from differences in school-level factors (e.g., financial resources, leadership quality) and time-varying factors that affect test performance at the school level

(A note on *panel data* and *cohort data*: In annotation 23, Rivkin, Hanushel, and Kain (2004) used the term *cohort data*. The definitions of these two concepts are not synonymous: A *panel study* involves selecting a sample at the outset of the study and then at each subsequent data-collection point, surveying the same sample, whereas a *cohort study* involves a different sample at each data-collection point from a population that remains constant (Gall, Gall, & Borg, 2007).

Key Findings

- There are large differences in quality among teachers within schools.

- It is estimated that a one-standard-deviation increase in teacher fixed effects raises student test scores by approximately 0.1 standard deviations in reading and math on nationally standardized distributions of achievement (p. 250).

- Teaching experience significantly raises student test scores for both reading subject areas (e.g., vocabulary and reading comprehension) and a math subject area (i.e., computation, but not math concepts). On average, ten years of teaching experience can raise reading test scores by approximately 0.17 standard deviations. For mathematics subject areas, the effects of experience are smaller. The first two years of teaching experience have a mild influence in raising scores in math computation. However, subsequent years of experience appear have no important association with test scores.

- Implications
  - Raising teacher quality may be a key instrument in improving student outcomes.

- Policies that reward teachers based on credentials may be less effective than policies that reward teachers based on performance.

Rowan, B., Chiang, F., & Miller, R. J. (1997). Using research on employees' performance to study the effects of teachers on students' achievement. *Sociology of Education, 70,* 256–284.

Overview

A general model of employees' performance, derived from the literature on organizational-industrial psychology, suggests that the effects of teachers on student achievement can be explained by three general classes of variables: teachers' ability, motivation, and work condition. These three classes of variables are hypothesized to have either additive or multiplicative effects on teachers' performance. The purpose of this study was to test this model. Specifically, this study attempted to address the following research questions:

♦ How have educational researchers conceptualized and measured the general constructs of teachers' ability and motivation?

♦ Are there direct effects of teachers' ability and motivation on students' achievement?

♦ Is there any evidence that teachers' ability and motivation interact to produce students' achievement? That is, are the relationships of ability and motivation to teachers' performance additive ($P=f[A+M]$) or multiplicative ($P=f[A*M]$)? (In an additive relationship, two variables are independent, while in a multiplicative relationship, two variables are interactive. In this case, if the teacher performance is a function of ability times motivation, teachers with high ability would not have a high performance unless they also have high motivation.)

♦ How do work situations affect teaching performance? Are the effects additive ($P=f[A+M+S]$), or do different situations make the relationship between ability/motivation and job performance vary ($P=f[A*S]$, $P=f[M*S]$)? (p. 267)

Methods

In this study, student achievement data on eighth grade through tenth grade math were drawn from the longitudinal files of the *National Education Longitudinal Study of 1988* (NELS:88).

Teachers' ability is determined by three measures: (1) Teacher's score on the math quiz included in NELS:88. The NELS teacher questionnaire contained a single item that was designed to measure teachers' mathematical knowledge. (2) Whether or not a teacher had majored in math in undergraduate and/or graduate school. (3) Teachers' ability in using higher-order thinking instruction.

Teachers' motivation is measured by (1) teachers' general force of motivation, which is assessed by items developed to measure three closely related constructs—teachers' self-efficacy, outcome expectations, and locus of control; (2) teachers' expectations for students to go to college.

Work conditions are measured by (1) teachers' responses to questionnaire items assessing the extent of (a) *teachers' control over decision making*, (b) *staff collaboration*, (c) *supportive leadership* in working environments; (2) principals' responses to items assessing whether the school is implementing (a) *the use of interdisciplinary teams*, (b) *a school-within-a-school structure*, (c) *the use of flexible class scheduling*, and (d) *the use of common planning periods for teams of teachers*.

Statistical analysis

Two-level hierarchical linear model (HLM) with data on students included at level 1 and school-related data included at level 2.

Findings

- Generally, the findings provide preliminary support for the hypothesized model that teaching performance is a function of teachers' ability, motivation, and work situation. However, effect sizes of variables measured in these three domains were fairly small. They tend to raise students' achievement by less than 0.10 standard deviations.

- The analyses revealed that teachers' knowledge of subject matter and expectancy motivation have direct effects on students' achievement in mathematics.

- Students whose mathematics teachers answered the math quiz item correctly had higher levels of achievement on the NELS math test than did those whose teachers answered the question wrong. (p. 269)

- Students whose mathematics teachers place more emphasis on higher-order thinking instruction *do not* have higher levels of mathematics achievement than those whose teachers place less emphasis on high-order thinking instruction.

- Students whose teachers have a higher general force of motivation do not have higher levels of achievement than do students whose teachers have a lower general force of motivation. However, teachers' student-specific expectancy motivation does have a statistically significant effect on students' achievement. Specifically in this study, students whose mathematics teacher expects the students to go to college outperform students whose teacher does not expect them to go to college by approximately 0.07 standard deviations. That means that students whose teachers have higher outcome expectations for them have higher levels of mathematics achievement than do students whose teachers do not hold such expectations for them.

♦ Among all the school restructuring variables examined in this study, only two had statistically significant effects on student achievement: Students who attended schools where teachers reported more *control over decision making* and shared *common planning periods* had higher levels of mathematics achievement (but the effects were very small). (p. 271)

♦ The effects of teachers' ability and motivation on students' achievement are additive (rather than multiplicative).

♦ The effects of school restructuring and effects of teachers' ability and motivation are additive too. (That means school restructuring did not interact with/condition/affect the effects of teachers' ability and motivation.)

♦ The school-level variable that had the largest effect on students' achievement was *the average ability of students* in a school.

♦ The effects of the teaching variables on students' achievement are especially substantive in schools with high proportions of low-achieving students.

  • A student in a low-ability school (i.e., one standard deviation below average) who is assigned to a mathematics teacher with solid content knowledge experiences only half the disadvantage of being in a low-achieving school, as compared with a similar student in a similar school who was assigned to a mathematics teacher who does not have solid content knowledge.

  • A student in a low-ability school who is assigned to a teacher with a degree in mathematics can make up about one-third of the disadvantage of being in a low-achieving school, as compared with a similar student in a similar school who was assigned to a teacher who does not have a degree in mathematics.

- The NELS data show that roughly 20 percent of the students in low-ability schools are assigned to mathematics teachers who do not have a degree in mathematics, do not have solid knowledge on subject matter, and do not expect the students to go to college.

Rowan, B., Correnti, R., & Miller, R. J. (2002). What large-scale, survey research tells us about teacher effects on student achievement: Insights from the *Prospects* study of elementary schools. *Teachers College Record, 104*(8), 1525–1567.

Overview

The purpose of this paper is to discuss conceptual and methodological issues that arise when educational researchers use data from large-scale survey research to examine the effects of teachers and teaching on student achievement (p. 1525):

- Why do different statistical models lead conflicting estimates on the overall magnitude of teacher effects on student achievement?

- Why do teachers impact on student achievement? What is the source of teacher effects?

Methods

This study used student achievement data on reading and math from grades 1 through 6. The data were drawn from *Prospects: The Congressionally Mandated Study of Educational Growth and Opportunity 1991–1994.*

Statistical Analysis

Three-level hierarchical linear model (HLM).

Findings

- Different statistical models would lead to widely varying interpretations about the overall magnitude of teacher effects on student achievement.

- Using a three-level, cross-classified, random effects model developed by the authors for this study (this model uses student gain scores, controls for student background variables, and is perceived to be relatively more valid and reliable), the findings demonstrated that the classroom to which students are assigned in a given year accounts for roughly 60 to 61 percent of the variance in students' academic growth in reading achievement and

50 to 72 percent of the variance in students' academic growth in mathematics achievement. This means teacher has an effect size of 0.77 to 0.78 for reading growth, and 0.72 to 0.85 for mathematics growth. These effects are both statistically significant and substantively important. Teacher effects can also be translated to amount of student learning: a classroom one standard deviation higher than another in teacher quality would produce about 2.13 months of added mathematics growth for a student during a calendar year.

♦ The findings of this model also indicated that classroom effects have only a moderate degree of consistency across difference subjects (i.e., reading and mathematics in this case), with correlation ranging from 0.30 to 0.47. This means that a given teacher may vary considerably in effectiveness when teaching different subjects or even different content areas within the same subject.

♦ The classroom effects are also influenced by different groups of pupils. Social background variables (socioeconomic status, gender, and minority status in this study) influence the annual achievement gains across classrooms, with the effects being larger at lower grades (especially in reading) than upper grades.

♦ What accounts for such classroom-to-classroom differences in achievement? The author used a well-known process-product paradigm to capture the effects the various aspects of teacher and teaching. This framework classifies related variables into four types: (1) *product variables*—"defined as the possible outcomes of teaching, including student learning"; (2) *process variables*—"defined as properties of the interactive phase of instruction, i.e., the phase of instruction during which students and teachers interact around academic content"; (3) *presage variables*—"defined as properties of teachers that can be assumed to operate prior to, but also to have an influence on, the interactive phase of teaching"; and (4) *context variables*—"defined as variables that can exercise direct effects on instructional outcomes, condition the effects of process variables on product variables, or both" (p. 1538).

  • Presage variables (p. 1541)

    ▪ In elementary grade-level reading, teachers' degree status or certification status are not associated with the growth in students' achievement. But teacher experience is a positive predictor students' achievement gains, the with an effect size of 0.07 for early grades and 0.15 for later grades.

- In elementary grade-level mathematics, teachers' certification in mathematics has no effects on student achievement growth. Teachers' years of experience have positive effects on growth in student achievement, but only for the later grades, with an effect size of 0.18. Students who are taught by a teacher with an advanced degree in mathematics have lower rates of growth than those who are taught by a teacher not having a mathematics degree, with an effect size of −0.25. That implies in comparison with holding an advanced degree and having solid content knowledge, the ability to represent this kind of content knowledge and translate it into effective instruction and student learning is much more important.

- Teaching processing variables
  - Time on task/active teaching
    ◆ Teachers' self-reports about time spent in instruction and teaching modalities have no significant impact on students' growth in reading or mathematics achievement.

    ◆ The time spent by students in working alone (where teachers are not active agents of instruction) has negative effects on reading growth, with an effect size of −0.09, and no significant effects on mathematics growth.

    ◆ For both reading and mathematics, the percentage of time spent in whole-class instruction has significant positive effects on student learning growth, with an effect size of 0.09 for reading and 0.12 for mathematics.

  - Opportunity to learn/content covered
    ◆ When looking at reading as composed of three curricular dimensions—word analysis, reading comprehension, and writing—the effect size of coverage on word analysis skills is 0.10; the effect size of comprehension is 0.17; and the effect size of writing is 0.18.

    ◆ In mathematics, the effect of content coverage on early grades was not statistically significant, but was significant for upper elementary grade, with an effect size of 0.09. (p. 1549)

- Thus, various (presage and process) characteristics of teachers and their teaching account for the classroom-to-classroom differences in instructional effectiveness, including teacher experience, use of whole-class instruction, and patterns of content coverage, with effect sizes ranging from 0.10 to 0.20. These small instructional effects may be combined to produce variance in classroom effectiveness.

♦ More discussions on large-scale survey research

- Readers should be cautious about the using statistical significance as the single standard to judge the impact of teacher and teaching variables. In large-scale survey research, the large sample size can make very tiny effects statistically significant.

- Although the variance decomposition models are useful in identifying the natural variation in classroom/teacher effectiveness, they cannot inform policy makers and educators why some classrooms are more effective than others. Future research in this field needs to look into classroom and directly examine teachers' instruction.

Sanders, W. L., & Horn, S. P. (1997). *Cumulative effects of inadequate gains among early high-achieving students.* Paper presented at the Sixth Annual National Evaluation Institute, Muncie, IN.

Overview

The analysis of TVAAS (Tennessee Value-Added Assessment System) on longitudinal student achievement data revealed that students at the highest level of achievement are making fewer academic gains than lower-achieving students in a large percentage of Tennessee schools, especially those located in metropolitan areas. The cumulative effects of disproportionate lower-effectiveness teachers assigned to black students could be a partial explanation for the widening achievement gap between black and white student populations. The analysis of student academic progress data in two metropolitan areas of Tennessee indicated that high-achieving black students had deflated academic growth as a result of schools failing to provide the appropriate growth opportunities.

Methods

The article reviews the application of the Tennessee Value-Added Assessment System (TVAAS) as a statistical tool.

Key Findings

♦ The least-effective teachers were ineffective to students of *all* achievement levels. The average teachers can facilitate the achievement gains with lower-achieving students, but not the student achievers of higher level. The highly effective teachers are generally effective to *all* student achievement levels. As teacher effectiveness increased, their effectiveness with students in the lower academic levels increase, but only highly effective teachers are effective with high-achieving students. (For more information, refer to Sanders and Rivers, 1996.)

♦ In the Tennessee school system, black students are disproportionately assigned to the least-effective teachers. However, when black students and white students are assigned to teachers of comparable effectiveness, they make comparable academic gains. The cumulative effects of the unequal pattern in assigning students to teachers account partially for the achievement gap between black and white student populations.

♦ The analysis of student academic progress data in two metropolitan areas of Tennessee indicated that high-achieving black students had a retarded academic growth rate because of schools failing to provide the appropriate growth opportunities.

Sanders, W. L., & Horn, S. P. (1998). Research findings from the Tennessee Value-Added Assessment System (TVSSA) databases: Implications for educational evaluation and research. *Journal of Personnel Evaluation in Education, 12*(3), 247–256.

Overview

The Tennessee Value-Added Assessment System (TVAAS) uses a massive database to link student achievement to particular schools and teachers longitudinally. It uses a mixed-model method to determine the effectiveness of school systems, schools, and teachers based on student achievement gains over time. Research using the TVAAS database shows that race, socioeconomic level, class size, and classroom heterogeneity are poor predictors of student academic growth. Rather, the most important factor impacting student academic progress is teacher effectiveness. The research also indicates that teachers' impact on student achievement is both residual and cumulative, and there is little evidence that subsequent effective teachers can remediate the negative effects of ineffective ones.

Methods

This article presents a summary of and an argument for the application of the Tennessee Value-Added Assessment System.

Key Findings/Recommendations

Summary of TVAAS

TVAAS uses statistical mixed-model methodology to enable a multivariate, longitudinal analysis of student scale scores. TVAAS can provide important information for summative evaluation by examining the effectiveness of schools systems, schools, and teachers in helping student achieve average academic gain. TVAAS could also serve as a data source for formative evaluation. School systems, schools, and teachers receive reports detailing their effectiveness with students of different achievement levels so that they can make timely adjustments with curricula, pedagogy, and special programs. The feedback from TVAAS could also troubleshoot the underachieving grade or subject area, so that efforts and resources could be more efficiently allocated.

Impact of Teacher Effectiveness on Student Performance

The authors reviewed empirical studies that used TVAAS data to examine the factors impacting students' academic growth. Some significant findings include:

♦ Cumulative gains in student achievement are found to be unrelated to the racial composition of schools or the percentage of students receiving free and reduced-price lunches.

♦ Teacher effectiveness is the dominant factor influencing student academic growth.

♦ Classroom context variables of heterogeneity among students have relatively little influence on academic gain.

♦ Student ability level also has a significant impact on student academic progress, but students with the highest academic performance make the lowest gains.

♦ Teacher effects on student achievement are both cumulative and residual. Subsequent assignment of effective teachers cannot offset the effects of prior ineffective ones.

♦ Ineffective teachers are ineffective with all students, regardless of their prior achievement level.

♦ As the level of teacher effectiveness increases, lower-achieving students are first to benefit, followed by average students, and, lastly, by students considerably above average. Only the most effective teachers achieved excellent academic progress with the highest-performing students.

♦ The residual effects of both effective and ineffective teachers are measurable two years later, regardless of the effectiveness of subsequent teachers.

Because teacher effects were found to be the most significant predictor of student academic growth, a meaningful teacher evaluation system should include student learning data. And any evaluation that does not look into effects the schools systems, schools, and teachers have on student academic growth is limiting its ability in achieving educational improvement.

Sanders, W. L., & Rivers, J. C. (1996, November). *Cumulative and re-sidual effects of teachers on future student academic achievement.* Knoxville, TN: University of Tennessee Value-Added Research and Assessment Center.

Overview

The Tennessee Value-Added Assessment System (TVAAS), designed by William Sander, is a method for investigating the cumulative effects of individual teachers on the rate of student academic growth. This study used the TVAAS database to investigate the cumulative and residual teacher effects on student achievement in mathematics as the students progressed from grade 3 to grade 5.

Methods

The Tennessee Value-Added Assessment System (TVAAS) requires three key components: (1) a testing process that produces scaled student achievement scores; (2) a large-scale, longitudinal database; and (3) a statistical process that conduct a multivariate, longitudinal analysis to produce unbiased and efficient estimates of the desired effects.

Key Findings

♦ Teacher effect on student achievement is cumulative. With an even start at the second grade, differences in student achievement of 52 to 54 percentile points were observed as a result of two extreme teacher sequences after only three years (low-low-low sequence versus high-high-high sequence).

♦ Teacher effect on student achievement is residual. A comparison of the low-low-high and high-high-high sequences revealed that there was a difference of 13 percentile points. Residual effects of relatively ineffective teachers from prior years can still be measured in subsequent achievement scores and could not be compensated even by assigning students to an effective teacher in a subsequent year.

♦ There is no significant interaction between teachers of different effectiveness levels over grades. An effective teacher receiving students from a relatively ineffective teacher can still facilitate excellent achievement gains in the students, despite the negative residual effects.

♦ The teachers in the lowest effective groups were ineffective with *all* achievement levels of students. Average teachers facilitated achievement gains with lower-achieving students, but not higher-achieving students. Highly effective teachers are generally effective with *all* student achievement levels.

Students of different ethnic groups (black and white students) respond equivalently within the same level of teacher effectiveness. Although the assignment of ethnic groups to effective teachers is slightly disproportionate (black students were overrepresented in groups with low teacher effectiveness), the achievement gains between the two ethnic groups were equivalent across different levels of teacher effectiveness.

Sato, M., Wei, R. C., & Darling-Hammond, L. (2008). Improving teachers' assessment practices through professional development: The case of National Board Certification. *American Educational Research Journal, 45*(3), 669–700.

Overview

An increasing body of literature reported that the National Board certification (NBC) process can help teachers be conscious of their teaching decisions and change their practices as a result. Previous interview/survey studies (participants' self-report) suggested that NBC can deepen teachers' conception of assessment. This study used direct measurements to examine how mathematics and science teachers' classroom assessment practices were affected by the NBC process and other similar professional development experiences.

Methods

Using a three-year, longitudinal comparison group design, evidence of changes in teachers' classroom practices were measured on six dimensions of formative assessment and at various points, including "three-year" means the year prior to pursuing NBC, a year of candidacy, and the postcandidacy.

The six dimensions of formative assessment include (1) views and uses of assessment; (2) range, quality, and coherence of assessment methods; (3) clarity and appropriateness of goals and expectations for learning; (4) opportunities for self-assessment; (5) modifications to teaching based on assessment information; and (6) quality and appropriateness of feedback to students. Each dimension was measured with a five-point rubric.

Samples included nine National Board candidates in middle school and high school science and mathematics area, and seven similarly experienced but non-National Board participants as a comparison group. Evidence of assessment practices were collected from a data packet consisting of videotaping of teaching, lesson plans, student work, and teacher interviews. Student and teacher surveys about teaching and assessment practices were conducted near the end of each of the three academic years of the study. Six of the teachers in the study (three NBC candidates and three non-NBC candidates) were selected for in-depth case analyses of their teaching practice.

Key Findings

- ◆ The National Board candidates began the study with lower mean scores than the comparison group on all six assessment dimensions, with overall mean scores of 2.62 and 2.90, respectively.

- ◆ During the certification year (the second year of the study), the National Board group made a substantial increase in assessment practices and had higher mean scores on all dimensions than those of non-National Board group, with statistically significant higher gains on four of the dimensions (view and uses of assessment; range, quality, and coherence of assessment methods; opportunities for student self-assessment; modifications to teaching based on assessment information).

- ◆ The National Board group largely maintained these assessment practices in the third year of the study and continued to demonstrate substantially higher scores, implying that they had likely incorporated assessment changes into their repertoire of practice.

- ◆ The assessment practices of most teachers in the comparison group changed little over the three years, except two teachers who reported having experienced professional development activities similar to NBC showed noticeable changes in practice.

- ◆ Analyses of student survey responses showed patterns in ratings that were consistent with trends in data packet scores.

- Case studies indicated that "National Board candidates identified changes in their conceptions of assessment as shifting from a focus on grading to the use of assessment for formative purposes. Hand in hand with that shift was a movement away from teaching for discrete facts to teaching for conceptual understanding and aligning those assessments better with learning goals" (p. 691).

- From the final reflective interviews with study participants, four main factors were identified as influencing change in the teachers' classroom practices: the National Board Certification process, other formal professional development opportunities, collegial interactions among teachers, and participation in the research study itself.

- Six of eight National Board candidates in this study cited the NBC process as a key factor that led to changes in their classroom practices. Candidates reported "the teaching standards of NBC provided a set of clear goals for practice and a practical sense of what constituted those goals" (p. 691). The NBC standard for "assessment" defines assessment practice as "the collection of information from a variety of sources and the use of that information to inform teachers' instructional decisions" (p. 692). This standard introduced them to new ways of viewing the role that assessment plays in their everyday instructional interactions. They also reported the portfolio requirements of NBC brought assessment practices into sharper focus, which prompted them to ask for evidence of learning and prompted specific, systematic attention to student learning (p. 692).

- "Teachers' classroom teaching practices can be influenced by professional activities that allow them the opportunity to closely examine their own practice" (p. 694).

Stronge, J. H., Ward, T. J., Tucker, P. D., Hindman, J. L., McColsky, W., & Howard, B. (2008). National Board certified teachers and non-National Board certified teachers: Is there a difference in teacher effectiveness and student achievement? *Journal of Personnel Evaluation in Education, 20*(3–4), 185–210.

Overview

Student achievement data from four North Carolina school districts (urban, suburban, and rural) were analyzed to determine the effectiveness of

National Board certified teachers (NBCTs) and non-National Board certified teachers. NBCTs were found to be slightly more effective in promoting student achievement than the non-Board certified teachers, but the difference was not statistically significant. In a followup study, fifty-three teachers participated in case analyses of effective teaching practices, consisting of interview, surveys, artifact selection, and classroom observations. Teaching practices of National Board certified teachers (NBCTs) were compared with their non-Board certified peers who produce high levels of student achievement (top-quartile teachers) and who produce lower levels of student achievement (bottom-quartile teachers). Identified non-NBC top-quartile teachers were found to be significantly better in selected nonacademic areas, such as classroom management and personal qualities, than both bottom-quartile teachers and NBCTs. No difference was found in the areas of instruction and assessment.

Methods

The hierarchical linear model (HLM) was used to determine teacher effects on student learning in mathematics and reading.

Instruments used in the study included:

- ◆ Teacher Sense of Efficacy Scale;

- ◆ Classroom Events Record as a record of teacher structured activities;

- ◆ Questioning Techniques Analysis Chart as a guide to categorize teacher/student questions based on Bloom's taxonomy;

- ◆ Student Time-On-Task Chart to record student engagement;

- ◆ Teacher Effectiveness Summary Rating Form, a rating scale to capture the types and degrees of effective behaviors exhibited by the observed teachers; and

- ◆ "Typical" Reading Comprehension Assignment as an instrument to investigate the quality of teachers' reading assignments.

Followup interviews also were used to determine quality of planning and assessment practices.

Threats to internal/external validity in the study included the small sample of National Board certified teachers in this study. Additionally, student achievement is just one educational outcome measure. Thus, the findings are not be generalizable to other important outcomes like motivation to lifelong learning.

The North Carolina fifth grade End-of-Grade Tests for reading and mathematics were used as measures of student achievement.

Key Findings

- Six student-level variables were taken into account in the analyses: gender, ethnicity, free lunch, ESL programming, special education status, and prior achievement. Ethnicity, free lunch, and ESL status had no significant relationships with student achievement in math and reading. Special education status was a significant predictor for math and percentage of whites was predictive for reading. Prior student achievement was a significant predictor for both math and reading achievement.

- There were no significant relationships between teacher demographic variables (e.g., years of service, ethnicity, pay grade) and teacher impact on achievement.

- ANOVA comparison indicated that NBCTs were slightly more effective in promoting student achievement than the non-Board certified teachers, but the differences were not statistically significant.

- No significant differences were found between NBCTs and non-Board teachers on the following variables: teacher sense of efficacy, cognitive level of questioning, student time-on-task, classroom management strategy, and nature of instructional interventions.

- NBCTs were stronger in the quality of their typical assignment as indicated by their engaging students in more cognitively challenging activities and giving clearer grading criteria.

- Based on the data collected by Teacher Effectiveness Summary Rating Forms, effective teachers (top quartile) were found to be significantly better in some nonacademic areas than less-effective teachers (bottom quartile) and NBCTs, such as classroom management, positive relationships, encouragement of student responsibility. No significant differences were found in the areas of instruction and assessment.

Wayne, A. J., & Youngs, P. (2003). Teacher characteristics and student achievement gains: A review. *Review of Educational Research, 73*(1), 89–122.

Overview

This article is a synthesis of existing studies that examine the relationship between student achievement gains and teacher characteristics. This review considered deliberately and systematically each study's qualities. Determinate relationships are synthesized for four major categories of teacher characteristics: college ratings, test scores, degrees and coursework, and certification status. The concluding section discusses general implications for policy makers and researchers.

Methods

Four criteria were developed to identify the studies that were included in this review:

- ◆ The studies must observe teachers' characteristics as well as the standardized test scores of these teachers' students.

- ◆ The data were collected in United States.

- ◆ The design accounts for students' prior achievement.

- ◆ The design accounts for students' socioeconomic status.

The authors considered groups of studies that focus on a particular teacher characteristic and then described explicitly each study. After that, the authors rendered a joint interpretation about whether teachers with that specific characteristic have a greater impact on their students' standardized test scores than teachers without that characteristic. Findings and implications for four categories of teacher characteristics were discussed: ratings of teachers' colleges, teachers' test scores, teachers' degrees and coursework, and teachers' certification status.

Key Findings

- ◆ Studies examining the rating of teachers' undergraduate institutions reviewed in this study generated following findings:

  - • Positive determinate relationships were found between student achievement and the rating of undergraduate institutions of sixth-grade and eighth-grade social studies teachers. No determinate relationship was found among twelfth-grade students.

  - • No relationship was discerned between student vocabulary score gains and teachers' college ratings.

  - • With white and black students, teachers from better-rated undergraduate institutions were more effective. Findings were indeterminate for Hispanic students.

  - • *Joint interpretation*: Some relationship exists between teacher college ratings and student achievement gains. Researchers were not always able to discern a relationship, but those relationships that were found were positive.

- *Implications*: Policy makers should encourage better screening of prospective teachers.

♦ Studies examining teacher test scores reviewed in this study generated following findings:

- Relevant licensure examination scores

  - Sixth graders learned less when their teachers scored higher on the National Teachers Common Examination (NTE). Indeterminate results were yielded for junior high and senior high school students.

  - School districts where teachers had higher TECAT (Texas Examination of Current Administrators and Teachers) scores were more likely to have higher gains in student test scores in reading, especially between third and seventh grades.

- Verbal skills scores

  - After teachers' experience and graduate education had been controlled, teachers' scores on a short verbal facility test explained some school-to-school variation in the gain scores.

  - No relationship was found between teacher's word test scores and student achievement gains.

  - Teachers' performance on the word tests affected their students' reading score gains but not their vocabulary score gains.

- Recent studies

  - Students whose teachers answered a high school-level mathematics test item correctly made larger mathematics gains between eighth and tenth grades, even after controlling for whether teachers held mathematics-related degrees.

  - Student reading scores gains from third grade to fourth grade were positively related to the average teacher ACT (American College Testing) score in school districts.

  - *Joint interpretation*: The seven studies involving teacher scores yielded divergent findings: determinate findings included five positives and two negatives. The most plausible reason for this divergence is the different controls used in the seven studies.

- *Implications*: More rigorous licensure examination for teachers. There is also a need for research on the relationship between student achievement and teachers' performance on tests currently in use.

♦ Studies examining teacher degrees and coursework reviewed in this study generated following findings:

- The available research results were mixed regarding the impact of teachers' degree level. Most studies were indeterminate and, among the four determinate findings, one was positive and three were negative.

♦ Recent studies on teachers' degrees

- Tenth-grade mathematics students whose teachers had master's degrees in mathematics had higher achievement gains than those whose teachers had either no advanced degrees or advanced degrees in nonmathematics subjects. In addition, students whose teachers had bachelor's degrees in mathematics learned more than students whose teachers had bachelor's degrees in nonmathematics subjects.

- Twelfth-grade mathematics students were found to learn more from teachers with mathematics majors and from teachers with master's degrees in mathematics.

♦ Research on teachers' coursework

- No relationship was found between fourth graders' mathematics achievement and the numbers of college-level, mathematics-related courses taken by their teachers.

- Controlling for teacher experience, tenth-grade students made more achievement gains when their mathematics teachers had more mathematics courses. Tenth- and eleventh-grade students were found to learn more in mathematics when their teachers had taken more mathematics courses.

- *Joint interpretation*: In mathematics, all determinate findings were positive, so it is possible to assert that students learn more from teachers having more mathematics-related coursework and degrees. However, in other subjects, student achievement results have been indeterminate or inconsistent (Goldhaber & Brewer, 1997, 2000; Monk & King, 1994).

♦ Studies examining teacher certification status reviewed in this study generated following findings:

- Mathematics students had higher achievement gains when their teachers held certification in mathematics as compared with holding no mathematics certification.

- Students' mathematics gains were higher when their teachers held standard certification in mathematics, as compared with the gains of those whose teachers held either no certification in mathematics (which includes teachers certified in other fields as well as teacher with no certification in any subject) or private school certification in mathematics.

- *Joint interpretation*: Mathematics students learn more when their teachers have standard mathematics certification.

Webster, W. J., Mendro, R. L., Orsak, T. H., & Weerasinghe, D. (1996). *The applicability of selected regression and hierarchical linear models to the estimation of school and teacher effects.* Paper presented at the Annual Meeting of the National Council on Measurement in Education, New York, April 9–11, 1996.

Overview

This article documented the efforts undertaken by the researchers in developing an accountability system that can accurately evaluate school and teacher effect on accelerating student growth. The system must contain the following features:

♦ It must be value-added;

♦ It must include multiple outcome variables;

♦ Schools must only be held responsible for students who have been exposed to their instructional program;

♦ It must be fair. Schools must be derive no advantage or disadvantage by starting with student with certain characteristics that have confounding impact on outcome; and

♦ It must be based on cohorts of students, not cross-sectional data.

The authors examined the applicability of two statistical systems, Ordinary Least Squares (OLS) and Hierarchical Linear Modeling (HLM), to identify effective schools and teachers.

Methods

The sample of this study was a longitudinal cohort which consisted of all students in the Dallas Public Schools who were in grade 3 in 1994 and grade 4 in 1995 and who had complete data in reading and mathematics.

Instruments

Iowa Tests of Basic Skills Reading and Total Mathematics subtests as measures of student achievement in reading and mathematics

Key Findings

- OSL models produced results that were very close to those produced by HLM models.

- Most OSL regression and HLM models used in this study accounted for more than 70 percent of the variance in student achievement in reading and mathematics.

- Results produced by all the OSL and HLM models in this study were extremely consistent, with correlations generally above 0.90.

- Results produced by all the models in this study were not correlated with individual student and aggregate school demographic variables (e.g., ethnicity, socioeconomic status, English proficiency). That means the models examined in the study were free from the biases relative to important school, teacher, and student-level contextual variables. In other words, schools derive no advantage/disadvantage from starting with minority or white students, high or low socioeconomic level students, limited or nonlimited English proficient students, or a high or low mobile student body (p. 24).

- Taking all results into consideration, it is recommended that a two-level HLM model (student-school) is the appropriate model to determine school effects. An adjustment of shrinkage on the model can make it appropriate to determine teacher effects; thus, there is no need for two different sets (two-level and three-level) of equations. This is because "school effect is really an aggregate teacher effect in that, within schools, there was relatively great between-teacher variance in student residuals coupled with little within-teacher variance" (p. 25).

The authors summarized some major findings of previous studies conducted in Dallas Public Schools (p. 6) as follows:

- A statistical system using school means produce spurious results because they do not take into account the within-school variance.

- Analysis of unadjusted gain scores produce different results than those produced by regression and HLM models.

- Reporting of absolute test scores without any additional analysis produced results that were systematically biased against schools with higher than average percent of minority, poor, and black student populations and in favor of schools with higher than average white and economically advantaged populations. These results were very different from those produced by HLM and regression analysis.

- Longitudinal HLM and regression analyses using two years of individual student data for prediction without taking into consideration contextual variables produced results that were somewhat consistent with the HLM and regression models discussed in this paper.

Webster, W. J., Mendro, R. L., Orsak, T. H., & Weerasinghe, D. (1998). *An application of hierarchical linear modeling to the estimation of school and teacher effect.* **Paper presented at the Annual Meeting of the American Educational Research Association, San Diego, CA, April 13–17.**

This article documented the efforts undertaken by researchers in developing an accountability system that can accurately evaluate school and teacher effect on accelerating student growth. The researchers determined that the system must contain the following features:

- It must be value-added;

- It must include multiple outcome variables;

- Schools must only be held responsible for students who have been exposed to their instructional program;

- It must be fair. Schools must derive no advantage or disadvantage by starting with students with certain characteristics that have a confounding impact on outcomes; and

- It must be based on cohorts of students, not cross-sectional data (pp. 2–3). (The authors pointed out that "the backbone of most state accountability systems is unadjusted test scores or student gain scores, often not even based on cohort data" p. 10.)

The authors reviewed several statistical models that meet these five parameters. "These models are designed to isolate the effects of a school's or teacher's practices on important student outcomes. The school effect can be conceptualized as the difference between a given student's performance in a particular school and the performance that would be expected if that student had attended a school with similar context but with practice of average effectiveness. The teacher effect can be conceptualized similarly at the teacher level" (p. 3). After having evaluated these models with certain criteria (i.e., goodness of fit: r^2), the authors concluded that:

- The two-stage, two-level student–school hierarchical linear modeling (HLM) is the model of choice for estimating school effect;

- The two-stage, two-level student–teacher HLM is the model of choice for estimating teacher effects.

HLM models seem to be the most appropriate methodology for adjusting the effects of student and school demographic variables, as they produce effectiveness indices that are not correlated with student level and school level contextual variables.

Bryk, et. al. (1988) cited four advantages of HLM over regular linear models (p. 5 of this article):

- It can explain achievement and growth as a function of school-level or classroom-level characteristics while taking into account the variance of student outcomes within schools or classrooms.

- It can model the effects of student characteristics, such as gender, race/ethnicity, or socioeconomic status, on achievement within schools or classrooms and then explain differences in these effects between schools and classrooms using school or classroom characteristics.

- It can model the between and within group variance at the same time and, thus, produce more accurate estimates of student outcomes.

- It can produce better estimates of the predictors of student outcomes within schools and classrooms by using information about these relationships from other schools and classrooms.

Despite the promise of HLM for predicting school and teacher impact on student learning, it is not free of concerns, the authors summarized the concerns raised in the extant literature and proposed solutions to address them.

Concerns	Solutions
The difficulty in measuring the long-term development of skills that may not be measured in year-to-year growth patterns.	Longitudinal growth curves or, alternatively, relationships based upon two years of data can be formulated.
The assessment of diverse areas of achievement that do not have readily available standardized tests (e.g., how to assess the effectiveness of nonacademic area teachers?).	Criterion-referenced tests can be developed and used to assess diverse areas of achievement.
Programs that pull out students for remediation, programs that involve team-teaching, and programs with extensive use of instructional aides inhibit the estimation of an individual teacher's contribution to student growth.	Data can be provided at the team level rather than at the individual teacher level.
Norm-referenced standardized tests sample broad subject domains and are unlikely to match closely the curriculum in particular classrooms at particular times.	Measures in addition to norm-reference tests can be used.
Well-established, broadly applicable, and accepted achievement measures are not available in all the relevant areas of learning.	Constituents are primarily interested in basic skills. Measures of learning in music, art, and physical education can be developed.
Standardized achievement tests are unlikely to reflect the full range of instructional goals in their subject areas. Norm-referenced tests tend to ignore higher-order skills. Therefore, it is likely that products of superior teaching are not measured adequately or completely.	Criterion-referenced tests can be used to measure higher-order thinking skills.

Concerns	Solutions
Students' learning ability, home and peer influence, motivation and other influences are powerful in affecting achievement.	What the student brings to the classroom in terms of background variables can be statistically controlled, which account for 9 to 20 percent of variance in student achievement.
The statistical method used to control for nonteacher factors cannot take into account all relevant factors.	Authors' experience proved that major factors that affect student learning are gender, ethnicity, limited English proficiency, and free- or reduced-lunch status, and all of them can be controlled in HLM.
The regression-based techniques (i.e., need student scores of at least two successive years) involved in this model create a problem about "degrees of freedom" (or sample size), as the number of students for individual teachers is relatively small to start with, and likely to become smaller because of the mobility of the student population.	The primary worry is about the stability of the regression line of each individual teacher, and replication over several years is the best safeguard.

Note: The items identified in this table are either adapted from or taken as direct quotes from Webster, Mendro, Orsak, & Weerasinghe (1998), pp. 7–9.

Weerasinghe, D., Orsak, T., & Mendro, R. (1997, January). *Value added productivity indicators: A statistical comparison of the pre-test/post-test model and gain model.* **Paper presented at the annual meeting of the Southwest Educational Research Association, Austin, TX.**

Overview

In the era of accountability, public school systems must find valid and reliable procedures to identify effective schools and teachers, and uncover ineffective ones, as well, to help students grow academically. As a result, researchers have been modeling schools and classrooms to calculate productivity indicators that will withstand not only statistical review but also political criticism. Two main approaches have been developed to address this problem: (1) using pre- and posttest student scores and (2) using student gain scores. The strategy for estimating student performance projections from a pretest score with adjustments for covariates is becoming the standard for producing productivity indicators, but the remaining question is: Should we be modeling the students' posttest score or student growth, that is, gain.

Methods

A hierarchical linear model was developed for each of the above-mentioned approaches. The statistical outcomes of those models are School Effective Indices (SEI) and Classroom Effective Indices (CEI). A set of criteria was established to determine which approach is better.

Key Findings

Pretest/Posttest model and the Gain Score model are highly correlated and produce very similar results regarding both SEI and CEI. However, the Pretest/Posttest model is preferred over the Gain Score model because it is less statistically complicated.

References

Aaronson, D., Barrow, L., & Sander, W. (2007). Teachers and student achievement in the Chicago public high schools. *Journal of Labor Economics, 25*(1), 95–135.

Adams, M. J. (1990). *Beginning to read.* Cambridge, MA: MIT Press.

Akiba, M., LeTendre, G. K., & Scribner, J. P. (2007). Teacher quality, opportunity gap, and national achievement in 46 countries. *Educational Researcher, 36*(7), 369–387.

Allington, R. L., & Johnston, P. H. (2000). *What do we know about effective fourth-grade teachers and their classrooms?* Albany, NY: The National Research Center on English Leaning & Achievement, State University of New York.

Amrein-Beardsley, A. (2008). Methodological concerns about the education value-added assessment system. *Educational Researcher, 37,* 65–75.

Ballou, D., Sanders, W., & Wright, P. (2004). Controlling for student background in value-added assessment of teachers. *Journal of Educational and Behavioral Statistics, 29*(1), 37–65,

Barber, M., & Mourshed, M. (2007). *How the world's best-performing school systems come out on top.* London: McKinsey & Company. Retrieved from http://www.mckinsey.com/locations/ukireland/publications/pdf/Education_report.pdf.

Bembry, K. (1999, Summer). *Developing joint ownership within a teacher appraisal system.* Paper presented at the Eighth Annual National Evaluation Institute, CREATE, Traverse City, MI.

Bembry, K. L., Jordan, H. R., Gomez, E., Anderson, M. C., & Mendro, R. L. (1998, April). *Policy implications of long-term teacher effects on student achievement.* Paper presented at the 1998 Annual Meeting of the American Educational Research Association, San Diego, CA.

Borko, H., & Livingston, C. (1989). Cognition and improvisation: Differences in mathematics instruction by expert and novice teachers. *American Educational Research Journal, 26*(4), 473–498.

Callender, J. (2004). Value-added student assessment. *Journal of Educational and Behavioral Statistics, 29*(1), 5.

Carrier, D. (2007, August 29). *New brief identified specific school features linked to elementary achievement scores.* Retrieved from http://www.childtrends.org.

Carter, P. J. (2003). *A review of highly effective teachers in Hamilton County: Analysis of current trends and implications for improvement.* Chattanooga,

TN: Public Education Foundation. Retrieved from http://pef.ddngroup. com/.

Cloud, J. (2008, February 2). The science of experience. *Time*. Retrieved from http://www.time.com/time/health/article/0,8599,1717927–2,00.html.

Cohen, D. K., Raudenbush, S. W., & Ball, D. L. (2003). Resources, instruction, and research. *Educational Evaluation and Policy Analysis, 25*(2), 119–142.

Cumulative effect. (2009). In *The free dictionary by Farlex*. Retrieved from http://medical-dictionary.thefreedictionary.com/cumulative+effect.

Cumulative effects. (2009). In *Mondofacto online medical dictionary.* Retrieved from http://www.mondofacto.com/facts/dictionary?cumulative%20 effects.

Darling-Hammond, L., Holtzman, D. J., Gatlin, S. J., & Heilig, J. V. (2005). Does teacher preparation matter? Evidence about teacher certification, Teach for America, and teacher effectiveness. *Educational Policy Analysis Archives, 13*(42). Retrieved from http://epaa.asu.edu/epaa/v13n42/ v13n42.pdf.

Duffet, A., Farkas, S., & Loveless, T. (2008). *High-achieving students in the era of NCLB.* Washington, DC: Thomas B. Fordham Institute.

Eberts, R. W., & Stone J. A. (1984). *Unions and public schools: The effects of collective bargaining on American education.* Lexington, MA: Heath.

Education Trust. (2001). *Good teaching matters: How well-qualified teachers can close the gap.* Washington, DC: Author.

Eisner, E. W. (2004). Preparing for today and tomorrow. *Educational Leadership, 61*(4), 6–10.

Emmer, E. T., & Evertson, C. M. (1979). Stability of teacher effects in junior high classrooms. *American Educational Research Journal, 16*(1), 71–75.

Emmer, E. T., & Stough, L. M. (2001). Classroom management: A critical part of educational psychology, with implications for teacher education. *Educational Psychologist, 36*(2), 103–112.

Figlio, D. N. (2002). Can public schools buy better-qualified teachers? *Industrial and Labor Relations Review, 55*(4), 686–699.

Finn, J. D. (2002). Class-size reduction in grades K-3. In A. Molnar (Ed.), *School reform proposals: The research evidence* (pp. 15–24). Tempe, AZ: Education Policy Research Unit, Arizona State University.

Fuchs, L. S., & Fuchs, D. (2003). *What is scientifically-based research on progress monitoring?* Washington, DC: National Center on Student Progress Monitoring.

Fuchs, L. S., Deno, S. L., & Mirkin, P. K. (1984). The effects of frequent curriculum-based measurement and evaluation on pedagogy, student achievement, and student awareness of learning. *American Educational Research Journal, 21*(2), 449–460.

Gall, M. D. (2001). *Figuring out the importance of research results: Statistical significance versus practical significance.* Retrieved from http://www.uoregon.edu/~mgall/statistical_significance_v.htm.

Gall, M. D., Gall, J. P., & Borg, W. R. (2007). *Educational Research: An introduction* (8th ed.). Boston, MA: Allyn and Bacon.

Goddard, R. G., Hoy, W. K., & Hoy, A. W. (2004). Collective efficacy: Theoretical development, empirical evidence, and future directions. *Educational Researcher, 33*(3), 3–13.

Goddard, R. G., LoGerfo, L., & Hoy, W. K. (2004). High school accountability: The role of collective efficacy. *Educational Policy, 18,* 403–425.

Goldhaber, D. (2002). The mystery of good teaching. *Education Next, 2*(1), 50–55. Retrieved from http://www.hoover.org/publications/ednext/3368021.html.

Goldhaber, D. D., & Brewer, D. J. (1997a). Evaluating the effects of teacher degree level on educational performance. In W. J. Fowler (Ed.), *Developments in school finance, 1996* (pp. 197–210). Washington, DC: National Center for Educational Statistics, U.S. Department of Education.

Goldhaber, D. D., & Brewer, D. J. (1997b). Why don't schools and teachers seem to matter? Assessing the impact of unobservables on educational productivity. *The Journal of Human Resources, 32*(3), 502–523.

Goldhaber, D. D., & Brewer, D. J. (2000). Does teacher certification matter? High school certification status and student achievement. *Educational Evaluation and Policy Analysis, 22*(2), 129–145.

Gordon, R., Kane, T. J., & Staiger, D. O. (2006). *Identifying effective teachers using performance on the job.* Washington, DC: Brookings Institution.

Greenwald, R., Hedges, L. V., & Laine, R. D. (1996). The effect of school resources on student achievement. *Review of Educational Research, 66*(3), 361–396.

Gross, B., Booker, T. K., & Goldhaber, D. (2009). Boosting student achievement: The effect of comprehensive school reform on student achievement. *Educational Evaluation and Policy Analysis, 31*(2), 111–126.

Guin, K. (2004, August 16). Chronic teacher turnover in urban elementary schools. *Education Policy Analysis Archives, 12*(42). Retrieved from http://epaa.asu.edu/epaa/v12n42/.

Hanushek, E. A. (1997). Assessing the effects of school resources on student performance: An update. *Educational Evaluation and Policy Analysis, 19,* 141–164.

Hanushek, E. A. (2008, May). *Teacher deselection.* Retrieved from http://www.stanfordalumni.org/leadingmatters/san_francisco/documents/Teacher_Deselection-Hanushek.pdf.

Hanushek, E. A., Kain, J. F., & Rivkin, S. G. (1998, August). *Teachers, schools, and academic achievement.* Cambridge, MA: National Bureau of Economic Research. Retrieved from http://www.nber.org/papers/w6691.

Hanushek, E. A., Kain, J. F., O'Brien, D. M., & Rivkin, S. G. (2005). *The market for teacher quality*. Cambridge, MA: National Bureau of Economic Research. Retrieved from http://www.nber.org/papers/w11154.pdf.

Harris, D. N., & Sass, T. R. (2007). *Teacher training, teacher quality and student achievement*. Washington, DC: National Center for Analysis of Longitudinal Data in Education Research. Retrieved from www.caldercenter.org/PDF/1001059_Teacher_Training.pdf.

Hattie, J. (2003). *Teachers make a difference: What is the research evidence?* Retrieved from http://www.leadspace.govt.nz/leadership/pdf/john_hattie.pdf.

Haycock, K., & Crawford, C. (2008). Closing teacher quality gap. *Educational Leadership, 65*(7), 14–19.

Haynie, G. (2006, April). *Effective biology teaching: A value-added instructional improvement analysis model*. Retrieved from http://www.wcpss.net/evaluation-research/reports/2006/0528biology.pdf.

Heistad, D. (1999, April). *Teachers who beat the odds: Value-added reading instruction in Minneapolis 2nd grade*. Paper presented at the Annual American Educational Research Association Conference, April, Montreal, Canada.

Henig, J. R. (2008, December/2009, January). The spectrum of education research. *Educational Leadership, 66*(4) 6–11.

Hershberg, T. (2005). Value-added assessment and systemic reform: A response to the challenge of human capital development. *Phi Delta Kappan, 87*(4), 276–283.

Hill, H. C., Rowan, B., & Ball, D. L. (2005). Effects of teachers' mathematical knowledge for teaching on student achievement. *American Educational Research Journal, 42*, 371–406.

Hoff, D. J. (2007, December 19). "Growth models" gaining in accountability debate. *Education Week, 27*(16), 22–23.

Hoy, W. K., Sweetland, P. A., & Smith, P. A. (2002). Toward an organizational model of achievement in high schools: The significant of collective efficacy. *Educational Administration Quarterly, 38*, 77–93.

Hoy, W., Tarter, J., & Hoy, A. W. (2006). Academic optimism of schools: A force for student achievement. *American Educational Research Journal, 43*(3), 425–446.

Huang, F. L., & Moon, T. R. (2009). Is experience the best teacher? A multilevel analysis of teacher characteristics and student achievement in low performing schools. *Educational Assessment: Evaluation and Accountability, 21*(3), 209–234.

Jackson, A. W., & Davis, G. A. (2000). *Turning points 2000: Educating adolescents in the 21st Century*. New York, NY: Teachers College Press.

Jackson, C. K., & Bruegmann, E. (2009). *Teaching students and teaching each other: The importance of peer learning for teachers*. Cambridge, MA: National

Bureau of Economic Research. Retrieved from http://www.nber.org/papers/w15202.pdf.

Jordan, H. R., Mendro, R. L., & Weerasinghe, D. (1997, July). *Teacher effect on longitudinal student achievement.* Paper presented at the CREATE Annual Meeting, Indianapolis, IN.

Kunter, M., Baumert, J., & Koller, P. (2007). Effective classroom management and the development of subject-related interest. *Learning and Instruction, 17,* 494–509.

Kunter, M., Tsiam, Y., Klusmann, U., Brunner, M., Krauss, S., & Baumert, J. (2008). Students' and mathematics teachers' perceptions of teacher enthusiasm and instruction. *Learning and Instruction, 18,* 468–482.

Kupermintz, H. (2003). Teacher effects and teacher effectiveness: A validity investigation of the Tennessee value added assessment system. *Educational Evaluation and Policy Analysis, 25*(3), 287–298.

Le V., Lockwood, J. R., Stecher, B. M., Hamilton, L. S., & Martinez, J. F. (2009). A longitudinal investigation of the relationship between teacher's self-reports of reform-oriented instruction and mathematics and science achievement. *Educational Evaluation and Policy Analysis, 31*(3), 200–220.

Lee, V. E., & Burkam, D. T. (2002). *Inequality at the Starting Gate.* Washington, DC: Economic Policy Institute.

Leigh, A. (n.d.). *Estimating teacher effectiveness from two-year changes in students' test scores.* Retrieved from http://econrsss.anu.edu.au/~aleigh/.

Lockwood, J. R., McCaffrey, D. F., Hamilton, L. S., Stecher, B., Le, V., & Martinez, J. F. (2007). The sensitivity of value-added teacher effect estimates to different mathematics achievement measures. *Journal of Educational Measurement, 44*(1), 47–67.

Long, J. F., & Hoy, A. W. (2006). Interested instructors: A composite portrait of individual differences and effectiveness. *Teaching and Teacher Education, 22*(3), 303–314.

Lumpkin, A. (2007). Caring teachers: The key to student learning. *Kappa Delta Pi Record, 43*(4), 158–160.

Mendro, R. L., Jordan, H. R., Gomez, E., Anderson, M. C., & Bembry, K. L. (1998a, April). *Longitudinal teacher effects on student achievement and their relation to school and project evaluation.* Paper presented at the 1998 Annual Meeting of the American Educational Research Association, San Diego, CA.

Mendro, R. L., Jordan, H. R., Gomez, E., Anderson, M. C., & Bembry, K. L. (1998b, April). *An application of multiple linear regression in determining longitudinal teacher effectiveness.* Paper presented at 1998 Annual Meeting of the American Educational Research Association, San Diego, CA.

Monk, D. H. (1994). Subject area preparation of secondary mathematics and science teachers and student achievement. *Economics of Education Review, 13*(2), 125–145.

Monk, D. H., & King, J. (1994). Multilevel teacher resource of effects on pupil performance in secondary mathematics and science: The case of teacher subject-matter preparation. In R. Ehrenberg (Ed.), *Contemporary policy issues: Choices and consequences in education* (pp. 29–58). Ithaca, NY: ILR.

Muijs, D., & Reynolds, D. (2003). Student background and teacher effects on achievement and attainment in Mathematics: A longitudinal study. *Educational Research and Evaluation, 9*(3), 289–314.

Munoz, M. A. (2001). *Class size reduction in a large urban school district: A mixed methodology evaluation research study.* Louisville, KY: Jefferson County Public Schools. Retrieved from http://www.eric.ed.gov.

Munoz, M. A., & Chang, F. C. (2007). The elusive relationship between teacher characteristics and student academic growth: A longitudinal multilevel model for change. *Journal of Personnel Evaluation in Education, 20,* 147–164.

National Academy of Education. (2008). *Teacher quality: Education policy white paper.* Washington, DC: Author. Retrieved from http://www.naeducation.org/Teacher_Quality_White_Paper.pdf.

Nye, B., Hedges, L. V., & Konstantopoulos, S. (2001). Are the effects of small classes cumulative? Evidence from a Tennessee experiment. *The Journal of Educational Research, 94*(6), 336–345.

Nye, B., Konstantopoulos, S., & Hedges, L. V. (2004). How large are teacher effects? *Educational Evaluation and Policy Analysis, 26*(3), 237–257.

Odden, A. (2004). Lessons learned about standards-based teacher evaluation systems. *Peabody Journal of Education, 79*(4), 126–137.

Odden, A., Borman, G., & Fermanich, M. (2004). Assessing teacher, classroom, and school effects, including fiscal effects. *Peabody Journal of Education, 79*(4), 4–32.

Palardy, G. J., & Rumberger, R. W. (2008). Teacher effectiveness in first grade: The importance of background qualifications, attitudes, and instructional practices for student learning. *Educational Evaluation and Policy Analysis, 30*(2), 111–140.

Residual. (2009). In *Merriam-Webster online dictionary.* Retrieved from http://www.merriam-webster.com/dictionary/residual.

Rice, J. K. (2003). *Teacher quality: Understanding the effectiveness of teacher attributes.* Washington, DC: Economic Policy Institute.

Rivkin, S. G., Hanushek, E. A., & Kain, J. F. (2005). Teachers, schools, and academic achievement. *Econometrica, 73*(2), 417–458.

Rockoff, J. E. (2004). The impact of individual teachers on student achievement: Evidence from panel data. *The American Economic Review, 94*(2), 247–252.

Rockoff, J. E., Jacob, B. A., Kane, T. J., & Staiger, D. O. (2008, November). *Can you recognize an effective teacher when you recruit one?* Cambridge, MA: National Bureau of Economic Research. Retrieved from http://www.nber.org/paper/w14485.

Rose, L. C., & Gallup, A. M. (2007). The 39th Annual Phi Delta Kappa/Gallup Poll of the public's attitudes toward the public schools. *Phi Delta Kappan, 89*(1), 33–48.

Rothman, R. (2008, Summer). Developing human capital. *Voices in Urban Education, 20.* Retrieved from http://www.annenberginstitute.org/VUE/summer08/Rothman.php.

Rothstein, J. (2009). *Teacher quality in educational production: Tracking, decay, and student achievement.* Retrieved from http://www.princeton.edu/~jrothst/published/rothstein_vam_may152009.pdf.

Rowan, B., Chiang, F. S., & Miller, R. J. (1997). Using research on employees' performance to study the effects of teachers on student achievement. *Sociology of Education, 70,* 256–284.

Rowan, B., Correnti, R., & Miller, R. J. (2002). What large-scale, survey research tells us about teacher effects on student achievement: Insights from the *Prospects* study of elementary schools. *Teachers College Record, 104*(8), 1525–1567.

Safer, N., & Fleischman, S. (2005). How student progress monitoring improves instruction. *Educational Leadership, 62*(5), 81–83.

Sanders, W. (2000). Value-added assessment from student achievement data: Opportunities and hurdles. *Journal of Personnel Evaluation in Education, 14*(4), 329–339.

Sanders, W. L., & Horn, S. P. (1994). The Tennessee Value-Added Assessment System (TVAAS): Mixed-model methodology in educational assessment. *Journal of Personnel Evaluation in Education, 8,* 299–311.

Sanders, W. L., & Horn, S. P. (1997). *Cumulative effects of inadequate gains among early high-achieving students.* Paper presented at the Sixth Annual National Evaluation Institute, Muncie, IN.

Sanders, W. L., & Horn, S. P. (1998). Research findings from the Tennessee Value-Added Assessment System (TVSSA) databases: Implications for educational evaluation and research. *Journal of Personnel Evaluation in Education, 12*(3), 247–256.

Sanders, W. L., & Rivers, J. C. (1996, November). *Cumulative and residual effects of teachers on future student academic achievement.* Knoxville, TN: University of Tennessee Value-Added Research and Assessment Center.

Sanders, W. L., Saxton, A. M., & Horn, S. P. (1997). The Tennessee Value-Added Accountability System: A quantitative, outcomes-based approach to educational assessment. In J. Millman (Ed.), *Grading teachers, grading schools: Is student achievement a valid evaluation measure?* (pp. 137–162). Thousand Oaks, CA: Corwin Press.

Sato, M., Wei, R. C., & Darling-Hammond, L. (2008). Improving teachers' assessment practices through professional development: The case of National Board Certification. *American Educational Research Journal, 45*(3), 669–700.

Schacter, J., & Thum, Y. M. (2004). Paying for high- and low-quality teaching. *Economics of Education Review, 23*, 411–430.

Schalock, H. D. (1998). Student progress in learning: Teacher responsibility, accountability, and reality. *Journal of Personnel evaluation in Education, 12*(3), 237–246.

Schalock, H. D., Schalock, M. D., Cowart, B., & Myton, D. (1993). Extending teacher assessment beyond knowledge and skills: An emerging focus on teacher accomplishments. *Journal of Personnel Evaluation in Education, 7*, 105–133.

Sigler, D., & Kashyap, M. U. (2008, Summer). Human capital management: A new approach for districts. *Voices in Urban Education, 20*. Retrieved from http://www.annenberginstitute.org/VUE/summer08/Sigler.php

Stecker, P. M., Fuchs, L. S., & Fuchs, D. (2005). Using curriculum-based measurement to improve student achievement: Review of research. *Psychology in the Schools, 42*(8), 795–819.

Stronge, J. H. (2007). *Qualities of effective teachers*, 2nd ed. Alexandria, VA: Association for Supervision and Curriculum Development.

Stronge, J. H., Gareis, C., & Little, C. (2006). *Teacher quality and teacher pay.* Thousand Oaks, CA: Corwin Press.

Stronge, J. H., Ward, T. J., Tucker, P. D., & Grant, L.W. (In review). Teacher quality and student learning: What do good teachers do?

Stronge, J. H., Ward, T. J., Tucker, P. D., & Hindman, J. L. (2008). What is the relationship between teacher quality and student achievement? An exploratory study. *Journal of Personnel Evaluation in Education, 20*(3–4), 165–184.

Stronge, J. H., Ward, T. J., Tucker, P. D., Hindman, J. L., McColsky, W., & Howard, B. (2008). National Board certified teachers and non-National Board certified teachers: Is there a difference in teacher effectiveness and student achievement? *Journal of Personnel Evaluation in Education, 20*(3–4), 185–210.

Taylor, B., Pearson, P. D., Clark, K. F., & Walpole, S. (1999). *Beating the odds in teaching all children to read.* Ann Arbor, MI: Center for the Improvement of Early Reading Achievement.

Tomlinson, C. A. (1999). *The differentiated classroom: Responding to the needs of all learners.* Alexandria, VA: Association for Supervision and Curriculum Development.

Tucker, P. D., & Stronge, J. H. (2005). *Linking teacher evaluation and student learning.* Alexandria, VA: Association for Supervision and Curriculum Development.

U.S. Department of Education. (1998, April). *Research on the academic effects of small class size.* Retrieved from http://www.ed.gov/pubs/ClassSize/academic.html

U.S. Department of Education. (2001). *No Child Left Behind Act of 2001*. Washington, DC: Author.

Viadero, D. (2008a, May 7). Scrutiny heightens for "value added" research method. *Education Week, 27*(36), 1, 12–13.

Viadero, D. (2008b, May 7). "Value-added" pioneer says stinging critique of method is off-base. *Education Week, 27*(36), 13.

Walberg, H. J., & Paik, S. J. (1997). Assessment requires incentives to assess value: A review of the Tennessee Value-Added Assessment System. In J. Millman (Ed.), *Grading teachers, grading schools: Is student achievement a valid evaluation measure?* (pp. 169–178). Thousand Oaks, CA: Corwin Press.

Walls, R. T., Nardi, A. H., von Minden, A. M., & Hoffman, N. (2002). The characteristics of effective and ineffective teachers. *Teacher Education Quarterly, 29*(1), 39–48.

Wang, M. C., Haertel, G. D., & Walberg, H. J. (1994). What helps students learn? *Educational Leadership, 51*(4), 74–79.

Wayne, A. J., & Youngs, P. (2003). Teacher characteristics and student achievement gains: A review. *Review of Educational Research, 73*(1), 89–122.

Webster, W. J., Mendro, R. L., Orsak, T. H., & Weerasinghe, D. (1998). *An application of hierarchical linear modeling to the estimation of school and teacher effect*. Paper presented at the Annual Meeting of the American Educational Research Association, San Diego, CA.

Weerasinghe, D., Orsak, T., & Mendro, R. (1997, January). *Value added productivity indicators: A statistical comparison of the pre-test/post-test model and gain model*. Paper presented at the annual meeting of the Southwest Educational Research Association, Austin, TX.

Wenglinsky, H. (2002). How schools matter: The link between teacher classroom practices and student academic performance. *Education Policy Analysis Archives, 10*(12). Retrieved from http://epaa.asu.edu/epaa/v10n12/.

West, J., Denton, K., & Germino-Hausken, E. (2000). *America's Kindergartners: Findings from the early childhood longitudinal study, Kindergarten Class of 1998–99*. (NCES 2000-070). Washington, DC: U.S. Department of Education.

Westberg, K. L., Archambault, F. X., Jr., Dobyns, S. M., & Salvin, T. J. (1993). *An observational study of instructional and curricular practices used with gifted and talented students in regular classrooms* (Research Monograph 93104). Storrs, CT: University of Connecticut, The National Research Center on the Gifted and Talented.

Wright, S. P., Horn, S. P., & Sanders, W. L. (1997). Teacher and classroom context effects on student achievement: Implications for teacher evaluation. *Journal of Personnel Evaluation in Education, 11*, 57–67.